MEMORIES

'LEST WE FORGET

**Anthology,
Stories and Recipes
of Yesteryear**

Compiled by
Stanley Naylor

MEMORIES first published in Great Britain October 1996 by Stanley Naylor and John R. Walsh

Copyright © Stanley Naylor and John R. Walsh 1996

ISBN 0 9527846 0 2

British Library Cataloguing in Publication Data

All rights reserved. No part of this publication may be reproduced, stored in a retrieval system or transmitted in any form or by any means, electronic, mechanical, photocopying, recording or otherwise, without prior permission in writing from the publishers.

RAFA BOOK CLUB BOSTON
37 Chester Way
Boston
Lincolnshire PE21 7PR

> The Publishers have agreed that donations from every book sold, will be made to the following organisations by the trustees of the RAFA BOOK CLUB BOSTON.
>
> The Royal British Legion   £1.00
>
> The Royal Air Forces Association
> "Wings Appeal Fund"   £1.00

Printed by Inkline Printing Co. Ltd.
Amber Hill
Boston
Lincolnshire PE20 3RQ

Cover picture : An artists impression

PREFACE

I am privileged to have been asked to write a Preface to Mr. Stanley Naylor's book, so aptly entitled "MEMORIES". I do so as one of the earliest post-war members of The Boston Branch of the Royal Air Forces Association, in which I served as Chairman and then as President for a good many years, and also as a longstanding member of the Boston Brance of the British Legion, of which I was President for several years. Thus I have been well aquainted with the great service which Mr Naylor has given to local ex-service associations over the years.

Undoubtedly the most outstanding contribution which Mr. Naylor has made in his varied ex-service work has been the compilation and writing of the "SUPERSONIC", that well known and highly acclaimed 'Newsletter of the Boston Branch' of R.A.F.A.

Many have greatly enjoyed reading it's items of Branch news over many years, but what will remain in their memories for years to come were the various articles, poems, stories and recipes which made the Newsletter so useful and enjoyable.

I have little doubt that many of my fellow members, like myself, have put aside many issues with a view to re-reading them on some future occasion and now cannot put their hands on them!

This is one of the reasons why Mr. Naylor has compiled and published "MEMORIES", thus bringing together in one handy book some of the most interesting items, which made "Supersonic" so interesting.

This has been no easy task, but one which Mr. Naylor has cheerfully carried out and I am sure that he has been ably assisted by Mr. John Walsh, who has contributed a number of his own poems, which have been well appreciated over the years by many Ex-service personnel and their families.

I am sure that in this publication readers will find a whole variety of items which will interest them and recall to mind episodes from their own Service days and many other memories, be they happy or sad. However the crowning feature of this whole project is the provision that part of the net proceeds of sale are being shared with the Royal Air Forces Association and the Royal British Legion.

I find it very typical of the author that he should have added to the title of his Book those very important and significant words: "LEST WE FORGET".

I trust that the combined efforts of Mr. Naylor and those who have helped him will be crowned with success. I wish them well.

RAYMOND L. RINGROSE

INTRODUCTION

In this introduction, I wish to acknowledge all those authors and many friends, who have made this book of "MEMORIES" possible.

During my 15 years writing the RAFA Boston Branch Newsletter, I gathered a lot of material, such as poems, stories and recipes. Plus the Newsletter won awards both in the National and Area Newsletter Competitions. The material therefore is so brilliant and of such high quality, it would be a shame to hide it away in a filing cabinet, and should be recorded for posterity. Hence the reason for the book, it will also, hopefully, swell the coffers of the Royal British Legion and Royal Air Forces Association.

It was at first thought the book would be called "SUPERSONIC," but that name is too modern for the material it contains. "MEMORIES" is a much more appropriate name and reflects the contents more accurately.

The poems and stories cover a wide spectrum of subjects and experiences inspired by the writers during their days in the Service sharing a unique bond of comradeship. To those authors who did not serve in any of the Armed Forces, we are pleased to have you on board, because your contributions entwines the material of the veterans. A classic example is by David Stubley of L.A.R.G. with his stories of recovering crashed aircraft. Thank you David.

My thanks to John Walsh, who has written 21 poems surrounding the famous Lancaster Aircraft, also for joining me as co-publisher. Thanks also to other contributors of poems including: Denys Brown, Max Father, Ethal Taylor and the late Joe Dodsworth.

Thanks are also due to the authors of the stories, to RAFA members who supplied old English recipes, to the trustees elected by the two Charity Organisations who have formed the RAFA BOOK CLUB BOSTON to administer the proceeds from the sale of the book "MEMORIES." Special thanks to the proof readers, your help is very much appreciated, your English is better than mine!

I hope I have done justice with the material given to me and that the authors will be pleased with the result. Because if this book had not been written, all these fine poems and stories would have been completely forgotten. Now "MEMORIES" will be deposited in the British Library for everyone to read and enjoy.

Should there be any inaccuracies, then it will be appreciated if you will let me know, so that they can be rectified in future editions.

Enjoy reading the poems, each one telling its own story, and I'm sure the stories in the book will prove interesting.

Stanley Naylor, Past President of Boston RAFA.

Life member of the Royal British Legion.

P.S. The reader may not have been in any of the Forces during the second World War, but may have endured those years in civilian life, then you can be inspired by these words:

"I see the damage done by enemy attacks, but also see, side by side with the devastation and amid the ruins, bright and smiling eyes, beaming with a consciousness of being associated with a cause far higher and wider than any human or personal issue. I see the spirit of an unconquerable people".

Winston Churchill, April 1941.

LETHAL LADY

****

O watch her 'twixt the goosenecks,
On the flarepath rolling fast;
Towards night sky with tail fins high,
And a day's brief dusk long past.

Have you felt a hardstand tremble
To four Merlin's blasting roar?
And seen that tailwheel dancing
To the slipstream's rushing bore?

Ever viewed a Lanc on funnels
As she homed on a misty morn?
Maybe glimpsed her low on the downwind leg,
Heard her snarl at the breaking dawn?

Hell's Terror at night this Lady,
As lethal still by day.
For her beauty concealed grim purpose,
And the Lanc had a debt to pay.

John R. Walsh

****

HOME RUN

****

Begone the night for we bring her home,
   Far below us the cold North Sea;
Now dawn stands nigh in the paling sky
   And we fly with our spirits free.

Revive new hope now we live again,
   Gone the fear that haunts our flight;
Fades the threat of death as we guide her
   West and our faithful Lanc rides light.

We shall not dwell on our trip to hell,
   Far behind us the hostile sky;
Seven still fly strong to the Merlin's song
   And the miles to home run by.

John R. Walsh 1986

****

MEMORIES

****

It's Berlin tonight, the 'Big City' - that's right!
Mem'ries of dusk with light fading fast
That nerve-soothing fag that could be your last!
The jokes and forced humour, the latest duff rumour.

Dispersal and Lancs, high octane-full tanks.
The groups of tense bods who don't fancy the odds!
Sprog crews with the jitters; last rush jobs by fitters.
Flying rations and maps; those last minute flaps.

Battledress and warm boots; chute harness and chutes.
Young pilots and crews, beware the main spar's sore bruise.
That deadly bomb bay loaded earlier that day.
The Erks and the WAAFS, the Paddys and Taffs.

For it's Berlin tonight, the 'Big City' that's right!
It's muck sweat to Berlin; now the coughing of Merlins,
That song heard before with its shattering roar.
Watch the shimmering props; light gleams from turret tops.

Clear perspex and metal; young men in fine fettle.
Not eager to go but it's Berlin and so;
Mae Wests, chewing gum, oranges for some.
Coffee in flasks, oxygen masks.

Mirth that sounds forced, hot crackling exhausts.
Oil pressure and boost, engine noise scares rooks from roost.
Last moments to borrow, and will I see tomorrow.
For it's Berlin tonight, the 'Big City' that's right!
Recalling mem'ries so true from the Ops' that I flew.

John R. Walsh 1988

****

IMAGES OF HELL

****

Surprisingly, I felt no pain
But saw night's darkness
Seared by flame;
Before my eyes a fiery hell,
High octane's reek before we fell;
Upon my face, the kiss of fire,
The white hot lips of hate's desire.
When numbness fled
There came no tears,
Yet agony worse than all my fears.
Undreamed-of suffering
That would not cease;
How could a man beg Death's release?
Now where once a face,
A mask - no more!
Of mottled pink and white
To stare at, and abhor.

John R. Walsh, 1987

****

DAY TRIP

****

Clear blue skies with flak,
It's a daylight Op' today.
As far as my eyes can see there's Lancs;
And for some this trip's one way

With kites in the air as bold as brass, Jerrie has got us cold.
Roulette's the game and the Reaper will call;
Who's banking on growing old?

No shield of night to cover us,
With darkness still far away.
The target's in sight with Lancs going down,
And for someone there's hell to pay.

John R. Walsh, 1989.

****

LAST OP

****

She drags oily smoke like a banner
As we limp back home close to dawn.
Q-Queenie's dark trace on the paling sky,
As another day is born.

One Merlin riddled by shrapnel;
Prop feathered with one blade standing high.
And six fly for base in the early morn
But with death as the long miles creep by.

For flak caught us high above Essen!
White-hot steel and the buffet of blast.
Now our mid upper lies dead and it's certain
That this Op' is young Taffy's last.

He lies blood-soaked and still on the rest-bed;
And there's nothing that we can do.
From the moment the jagged shards found him,
Our gunner's brief life was through.

For there are ugly slashed rents in his turret.
The port outer's cowling's holed too
With prop blades edge on to the airflow.
Now can Skipper see us home true?

Far below us the cold North sea threatens
As we struggle due west on three.
It's Taffy's last run in the primal dawn light.
The Reaper has set him free.

John R. Walsh, 1994

****

A PRAYER FOR YOU

****

You told me not to worry,
That you'd always make it through.
You said to keep my chin up
And just say a prayer for you.

The young think they're immortal
With death far out of sight
But not for such as you though;
Death flew with you each night.

And Ops would be to Berlin
Or Dortmund or Cologne.
These fearful hours of hoping.
Each night I slept alone.

But many nights were sleepless
And I would lay forlorn.
For fate could keep me waiting
'Till another day was born.

But then the roar of Merlins
Would boom across the sky;
I'd try to count each Lanc safe home;
More often though I'd cry.

Then one morn they came to tell me
That you were overdue;
But later it was 'Missing'
For S-Sugar and her crew.

Now my crying is long over
Though I'll always know the pain
And my prayers will ever be for you
For you'll not come home again.

John R. Walsh, 1987.

****

ODDS AGAINST TOMORROW

****

Do you recall those days old pal
And remember as I do?
A sergeant's chevrons on our sleeves,
Bold white against proud blue?

Remember now those take-offs,
To sorties flak and hate
With "Watch that swing to port now Skip,"
And "throttle's through the gate?"

What about tense briefings
With terror at your guts?
Long musk-sweat trips to Berlin;
How sharp the memory cuts.

Then maps and weather,
Those bombing heights,
And "Watch out for the flak!"
Those wistful prayers on climb out,
"Dear God, may I come back!"

John R. Walsh, 1986

****

BEYOND THE WIRE

****

Walk the compound bomber boy
And hate its every yard;
The Jerries clipped your wings old son
A Kriegie's* life is hard

Pace along the hard-packed mud,
But not too near barbed wire.
Don't even dream of vaulting,
You would die from Mauser fire.

Step out nice and brisk then
It'll take your mind off food,
And do not mock your favourite Goon,
He's in a filthy mood.

Despair with every step lad,
No use to yearn for home
Barbed wire and guards to hold you,
There's not much chance you'll roam.

Next week a Red Cross parcel,
If Jerrie hands them out.
A bar of chocolate goes down well
When you eat next to nowt.

Tread the dusty compound,
Forget about that girl.
It's quite a while from now 'till then,
Did she make your head fair whirl?

There are air crew from all nations:
British, Canucks, Yanks.
Aussies, Poles and Kiwis;
Men of many ranks

Be thankful you survived son,
The Reaper passed you by,
But others weren't so lucky
For thousands had to die.

So fight to keep your chin up
And see the long months through,
Remember: when it's over,
Sweet freedom waits for you.

John R. Walsh, 1986.

*Kriegie is an abreviation of the German Prisoner of War - Kriegegefanganer.

****

FROM DARKNESS LEAD ME

****

I will remember this, one day.
Injured men who are but boys
Who bear the scars of heroes proudly
Like some badge of honour.

You lie for all the world
Like broken toys along my ward;
Enduring skin grafts, and the searing glare
Of new-burned flesh a'more,

The stifled cry of pain
That strikes my heart
And brings my silent tears afresh.
For he was also burned like you,
But I will see him no more.

John R. Walsh

****

REMEMBER

****

Remember us; we would ask you,
Through dawn and the break of day
And recall us then with your quiet prayers,
In the lofting sun's first rays.

Know that we bought your freedom,
But grieve not hard at the cost.
For better far we pay the highest price,
Than suffer your future lost.

Remember then, we would ask you,
Through sunset's last red glow.
And salute us all with the bugle's call
For the dawns that we'll never know

John R. Walsh

****

Night after night, young men would sally forth from tranquil rural Lincolnshire to take part in one of the most hazardous operations to be mounted against Nazi Germany. Young air-crews carried the power of Bomber Command against the Nazi Reich.
The odds against survival were fearful. No more than 1 in 4 would live to survive what was euphemistically termed "A First Tour of Operations." Lincolnshire, being Bomber County, was tragically the last home for not far short of half of them.

BADGE OF SHAME

****

Still a warrior through this day
But a coward come tomorrow,
These hours 'twixt now and morn'
My rack of shame and sorrow.

What shall I say to THEM?
Shall their reaction be,
Just scorn, disgust, sheer disbelief;
Or will they pity me?

No more will I command and fly
That Lancaster I love,
For fear of death and shattered nerves
Go ever hand in glove.

Must I bear a coward's brand
For I have given all.
I count the Ops' my log book shows
But they'll not understand.

For night on night I've known
What fear and death can be!
Through flak and hate, those alien skies,
Night's been no friend to me!

What of my brave young crew?
Will they too turn from me?
For I recall other missing crews;
Who'd know, and weep for me.

More - I fear the scorn of comrades,
Those men who know me well;
For I am not the only soul
Who's flown Lancs into hell.

Will Mum and Dad despise me,
Or maybe understand?
Shall they mourn the shame I bear,
Or gently take my hand?

I've given my all
Now there's no more to give,
So I guess this sets me apart.
But can they say; with all honesty,
That they never felt fear, for a start?

I know this is it,
And I'll stand all alone,
While they rip off
My brevet; unsewn.
Then they'll strip off my tapes
And brand me with shame;
And then it's a posting away.

John R. Walsh, 1986

****

Author's Note: LMF (Lacking Moral Fibre) applied to aircrew who 'cracked' under the strain, fear, and stress of continual Operations over enemy territory. Their refusal to fly on any further sorties, incurred the anger of authority. Their service documents were deliberately stamped, with the letter LMF. Their aircrew uniform brevet was stripped from them, leaving the easily discernible mark of the brevet, i.e. pilot's wings or airgunners AG. Then they were posted to another unit, as non-combatant. Such unfortunates usually ended up sweeping out hangars, or some other menial, soul-destroying duty. And the mark left on their battledress tunic jacket, easily identified by other airmen, showed what had befallen them. This was a deliberate policy to try to discourage 'nerves' or refusal to fly on Operations.
J.R.W.

ECHOES

****

There are sounds out there if you listen;
Sad voices from the past,
On the brooding silence of any 'drome
When the purpling dusk falls fast.

Walk soft past the crumbling Nissens,
Are there whispers on the air?
Does ghost meet ghost in the brief twilight?
Are pale phantoms murmuring there?

Lost spirits of the Commonwealth,
Empire and Allied kin.
Are they out of sight in the fading light,
Each night as the dusk draws in?

Stroll past the gaunt dark hangars,
Is that the reek of engine oil?
Do the shade of long dead riggers
Work on in their endless toil?

Walk on the windswept runways
Where once the Lancs sought flight,
Is the haunting song of the Merlin strong;
A pulse through the long sad night?

Traverse the long-stilled firing butts
Where no more the Brownings bark,
Would you dare the ghosts from yesteryear
Come the threat of the looming dark?

John R. Walsh, 1986

****

BROTHERS

****

We shared a common bond throughout those wartime years
For we were young and together, shared the doubts and fears of war.
How well we came to know that world within a world, wherein we lived,
And far apart from other fighting men who fought as we
did a common foe.

Vast was our arena. The swift darkening light at dusk.
The snarling roar of laden Lancs;
The on-rushing hours that claimed our youth,
The lethal night time skies; and we were so aware
That we might die before sweet dawn.

And so we knew death and lived o'er long with fear.
Although there were those amongst us that did not care!
But often, he who laughs the loudest fears the most.
So night after searing night we flew into Hell as brothers;
To find that the Reaper was our grinning host.

John R. Walsh

****

DAWN LIGHT

****

I walk alone through a morning mist
On the Wolds of Lincolnshire,
But why subdued in the breaking day
Was it thus in yesteryear?

Are they close to me those brothers
Who fell in days of yore?
Do you hold good watch young warriors
Though your big Lancs snarl no more?

Are you with me in the dawn light,
As I keep that vow I made?
While I walk with pride, are you at my side,
Or afar in some unmarked grave?

I come now as I promised;
A brief return to yesterday,
My yearning strong for old battle skies
As my last years rush away.

John R. Walsh, 1987

****

WAR DAYS

****

Don't go back they told me,
For you'll only find a grave.
The spirit that once inspired that field
Departed with the brave.
This 'drome deserted; this sad site
Knows only tractors maybe plough.
Windswept dispersals empty now,
Where our Lancs crouched, awaiting night.
Then, through days we hoped; the nights endured
With the 'morrow never ours secured -
For Ops', those hours of living hell,
The dawn we'd never dare foretell.
Our futures thrown on dice by fate
Dark angry skies that flamed with hate.
And bomber streams; the lethal flak,
Stricken Lancs with no way back.
And dying men who'd given all
With targets reached - or not at all.
Each night the fight to stay alive,
And which of us might yet survive?
War days I knew so long ago;
Of yesteryear and blue-clad youth;
How few survive from all that throng?
So many brave too quickly gone.
Those martyrs then of tender years,
Still only boys, but ever men.

John R. Walsh, 1988.

****

RETURN TO YESTERDAY

****

I went back to the lonely Wolds,
The Fens and the empty sky,
I saw the tall, gaunt elms,
Heard the calling rooks.
How time had passed me by!

Grass has grown on the runways,
In the hangars stand rusting ploughs.
The dispersal points were empty
Just starlings and grazing cows.

The Watch Office stood deserted,
Or maybe the ghosts of men
Stood and watched
While I walked remembering,
For I'd said, "I'll come back again."

The windsock hung in tatters,
Forlorn in the cold damp air,
Then I thought, `What does it matter?
There is no body here to care.

The crew huts were but ruins,
Rotting timbers and sagging floors,
Not a voice to break the silence,
Just the wind and the creaking doors.

Then I recalled these once were billets,
Full of life and the noise of men,
With the crackling roar of Merlins,
Or the whispering scratch of a pen.

So I stood quite still to listen.
Was there a message there for me?
In the shadows, would they remember?
Had they left me a sign to see?

If they had, it was too elusive,
Made dim by the veil of years
And I recalled all the purpose and courage,
'Till my eyes were blurred by tears.

I turned away downhearted.
This was not the field I had known.
Not the brave bold home of my memories.
Fool I was, for the years had flown.......

John R. Walsh, 1990

****

For all of them. For all 57,000 Bomber Command aircrew who never returned to base between 1939 and 1945. For all the young warriors who saw dusk but never saw dawn.

John R. Walsh, 1990

SEVEN MINUS ONE

****

Was it all that long ago,
Is it really two score years?
But we were nowt but youngsters then.
I can't believe they're here

There's Skip with Taffy, Jock and Pat;
As usual Pete's alone.
Cruel tragedy about young Mike;
He died above Cologne.

Here: all six of us together ;
No, seven minus one.
We vowed to this reunion
When that cruel war was done.

Yes; when that war was o'er we swore,
But not these forty long-drawn years:
I truly should have stayed at home,
Now my eyes are full of tears.

Well: just look at us old bomber boys;
Our bald heads and our pots
I notice Pete's the same as ever was;
And knocking back neat tots.

Take heed of Skipper supping ale
He's three sheets to the wind
His eyes so keen when we flew Ops'
Are looking rather dimmed.

But none of us is young, alas!
For time has passed us by,
In sleep, I hear the Merlin's song,
In dreams my battle skies.

We're sinking pints in same old pub
That welcomed us through war.
Then: we'd sing and laugh to blot out fear;
We shan't do that a'more.

Survivors yet the six of us
Alive to sup at beer,
We live to toast those other lads,
Those bods who can't be here.

How many tragic thousands -
Fifty? - maybe more;
And what a bloody price to pay,
But that's so true of war.

There's six of us together,
Or seven minus one.
So raise your tankards for them all:
And we seven minus one.

John R. Walsh, 1986

****

FATHERS - SONS

****

They were only lads I know;
My guess is that they'd say,
"That's so!"
Just names in chalk
Scrawled on that board,
But young faces from
My mem'ries hoard.

Loud voices ringing through this bar.
Jokes and laughter,
The haze of fags and smell of beer
A jar would help drown fear awhile.
They'd sing and joke,
I'd see them smile!

But then off guard they'd seem forlorn
With faces pensive, tired, and worn.
Fatigue and tension borne so well;
But each with his own tale of hell.

For depicted there was youth at war,
Just like their father's years before
"That war to end all wars " 'twas said.
But words come cheap; the dead stay dead

John R. Walsh, 1989

****

TORMENT

****

Once more in sleep my nightmare is terror;
And Fear is a flak-pocked sky!
My era is yesteryear and the days of Lancs,
Of cold cruel air where young men die.

Martyrs all alone in anguish.
The frigid sunlight of another killing day.
Now where the tumbling bombs seem to fall forever.
Yet so short is our time to pray.

Again I must endure the deadly dance of fate.
See flaming pirouettes of falling Lancs;
Espy slowly drifting snow white blooms of chutes
Amidst the lethal bursting flak flowers of a daylight raid.

And in my sleep must I, an ageing warrior now,
Still search for fighters seeking easy prey.

John R. Walsh

****

THE LION SLEEPS

****

Low cloud overcast above my head;
Your defiant voice bids me
Look up in quick surprise,
The sleeping afternoon's peace betrayed
As your instant shattering thunder
Splits the drifting Sunday sky.

And at once warm tears invade
To blur my eyes as I watch
Your angular threatening beauty
Proudly scorn a tranquil day.
Others ignore you, yet how could they know, or care
Why just I alone must stand and stare?

Lancaster:
You hustle through the hazy tenuous sky,
Evoke my fragmented past awhile and dazed,
I hear the angry snarling echoes of you slowly fade;
Yet though my eyes are wet, I smile, amazed.
But now my fretful mind again sees tracer
Streaking through an alien night,
The sudden burst of twinkling malevolent flak
Reaching to destroy your laden graceful night.

Then would I and those
Who crewed you surely die,
Soon listed missing,
Lost in deadly hostile skies.

Lancaster:
I quickly shrug those fearful nights
Of killing violence from my thoughts.
Let the fading trusty heartbeat of your Merlins
Keep faith with those who fell so young.
That I may rest, assured,
Knowing that The Lion only sleeps.

John R. Walsh, 1990

****

ADVANCE

****

Misty mountains rising,
Slithering, treacherous track.
Upward, ever climbing,
Sodden weary back.
Eyes alert, seeking,
Snipers in trees.
Mud, glutinously clinging,
Weakening shaky knees.
Ahead, grenades thudding,
Staccato rifle fire.
Enemy slowly retiring,
Leaving funeral pyre.
Hazy battle smoke,
Frenzied wailing cries.
Padre peaceful praying,
Youthful soldier dies.
Stretcher bearers clearing,
Wounded safely away.
Mournful bugle sounding,
Ending fighting day.

Author unknown but believed to relate to the First World War.

****

MEMORIALS

Memorials have been catalogued in various publications, but I think the one at the entrance to East Kirkby Aviation Centre merits a mention in this book. Mainly because of this poem that is inscribed on a stone beside the memorial.

OLD AIRFIELDS

****

I lie here still, beside the hill,
Abandoned long to nature's will,
My buildings down, my people done,
My only sounds, the wild bird songs.

But my mighty birds will rise no more.
No more I hear the Merlins' roar.
And never now my bosom feels,
The pounding of their giant wheels.

From the ageless hill their voices cast.
Thundering echoes of the past.
And still in lonely reverie.
Their great dark wings sweep down to me.

Laughter, sorrow, hope and pain.
I shall never know these things again.
Emotions that I came to know,
Of strange young men so long ago.

Who knows, as evening shadows meet.
Are they with me still, a phantom fleet.
And do my ghosts still stride unseen.
Across my face, so wide and green.

And in the future, should structures tall,
Bury me beyond recall.
I shall still remember them,
My metal birds, and long-dead men.

Now weeds grow high, obscure the sky.
O remember me, when you pass by.
For beneath this tangled leafy screen,
I was your home, your friend, "Silkscreen."

W. Scott Ex-630 Squadron.

****

This verse was found attached to a wreath of poppies at the foot of Theipvall Memorial on the Somme.

Your hand I cannot touch,
But God will take our message
To the one we loved so much,
Goodnight, God Bless.

Signed: Your loving daughter, Olive.

DAWN SERVICE

****

It's just a simple service in a country town I know,
When steady stars are paling and the sleepy earth wakes slow.
With grassy smell of morning and the bright dew on the lawn.
It's just a simple service in a country town at dawn.

There isn't any grand parade, or marching, or a band.
But just a little group of blokes who watch, and think, and stand.
There isn't any bugle there to play a sad "Last Post".
But from the mist of memories, the past steals like a ghost.

And all the intervening years the busy mind will bridge,
To deserts harsh, the beaches cold, the river, jungle, ridge,
To laughter, fear, a thousand things, the faces and the jokes.
And how it all comes back again just starting with the blokes.

It's just a simple service while the dawn is breaking red.
It's not the words a fellow hears, but those that stay unsaid.
It's not the glow of glory that the fleeting moments lend,
But just the recollection - in the morning of your friends.

by Max Father South Australia.

****

"Dawn Service" no doubt refers to a small Anzac ceremony in an Australian Town, if you close your eyes, it could so easily be anywhere you want it to be.

S.N.

During my tours of the Somme in France, I found this piece of poetry written on a stone in Newfoundland War Memorial Park, Beaumont Hamel.

Newfoundland Park embraces the ground over which the Newfoundlanders fought on the first day of July 1916, with a great loss of life. The land was purchased and the Park constructed under the direction of Lt. Col. T. Nance and R.H.K. Cochius Esq. Landscape Architect. The Park was then opened on the 7th June 1925 by Field Marshal Earl Haig, K.T., G.C.B., O.M.

        Tread softly here! Go reverently and slow!
        Yea, let your soul go down upon its knee,
And with bowed head, and heart abased, strive hard
        To grasp the future gain in this sore loss!
        For not one foot of this dank sod but drank
        Its surfeit of the blood of gallant men,
Who for their faith, their hope - for Life and Liberty,
        Here made the sacrifice - here gave their lives,
        And gave right willingly - for you and me.

        From this vast altar - pile the souls of men
        Sped up to God in countless multitudes,
        On this grim cratered ridge gave their all,
            And giving, won.
        The peace of Heaven and Immortality.
Our hearts go out to them in boundless gratitude;
        If ours - then God's; for this vast charity
All sees, all knows, all comprehends - save bounds,
        He has repaid their sacrifice; and we?
        God help us if we fail to pay our debt
        In fullest full and unstintingly!

John Oxenham

****

SOUNDS DOWN THE WIND

****

Silently he stood alone on the broken runway,
his thinning hair grizzled grey as the winter sky.
Down wind he turned and suddenly
alert his mind to sounds he cannot hear.
Out of the gloom came rumbling
four Merlins, roaring their defiance
away from the sun and into the black of Hell's mouth.
Again the excitement, apprehension,
comradeship's assurance, yet deep inside alone.
He sensed the nervous jokes, the crumpled fag,
the final pee in a group, behind the tail,
more superstition than physical relief,
the banter, the attention to details hid the fear.
The God-thanked exhaustion of a safe return.
"Finish your questions,
let's get the eggs and bacon and sleep"
Tomorrow will be soon enough
to mourn the missing. We're back,
unhurt until the next time.
He turned away a tearbrooked cheek.
But, alone, there were none to see.
Gone the Merlins' roar.
Gone! A casualty to time as he is.
Then the young airman,
Now, one of the grey old men,
Who in those potent and terrible years
fell in love with a winged machine
and still rave over her undimmed beauty.
Gentlemen! THE LANCASTER.
"God Bless Her"

By Denys Brown c 1989

****

HIGH FLIGHT

****

Oh! I have slipped the surly bonds of earth
And danced the skies on laughter-silvered wings;
Sunward I've climbed, and joined the tumbling mirth
Of sun-split clouds - and done a hundred things
You have dreamed of - wheeled and soared and swung
High in the sunlit silence. Hov'ring there
I've chased the shouting wind along, and flung
My eager craft through footless halls of air.
Up, up the long delirious, burning blue,
I've topped the windswept heights with easy grace
Where never lark, or even eagle flew -
And, while with silent lifting mind I've trod
The high untrespassed sanctity of space,
Put out my hand and touched the face of God.

****

'High Flight' was written by Pilot Officer Gillespie Magee, Jnr.
of No 412 Squadron RCAF
who was killed in a Spitfire on December 11th, 1941

THE "IMMORTAL FEW"

****

To eagles fallen, the glorious, the brave,
in a tidy churchyard or some unknown grave.
But memories are for veterans with their earthly toil,
cold clay their reward in our rich warm soil.

Back to an era nigh on fifty years,
life was for living as they diced with their fears.
And signed their honour in a clear sky,
a heritage of pride, to fight and to die.

Each to their fate, their Kismet had led,
on some foreign field their life force bled.
Just everyday "boys", every mother's son,
who loved and laughed then climbed into the sun,

Deed as the honour to accept their gift,
the wind 'neath our wings to Heaven will lift.
To meet those "Boys" in a dimension unknown,
those silent Heroes with whom you have flown.

Those Knights of the air who received their call,
to face the enemy and to give their all.
They left us a legacy through the barriers of time,
to transcend this life to immortality sublime.

To those young warriors who've seen the Lord's face,
the Victory is yours to receive now his grace.
To consummate their destiny, they've paid their earthly due,
and remain throughout Eternity, as the valiant "Immortal Few."

With pride,   *Jock Turner, Christchurch, N.Z.*

****

IN ST. CLEMENT DANES, THE STRAND, LONDON. THE CENTRAL CHURCH OF THE ROYAL AIR FORCE

Row upon row,
A nation's pride,
Row upon row,
The names of men who died.
Isle of tranquillity
Midst traffic's roar,
Banner emblazoned balcony,
Squadron crested floor.
Beating hearts draw near,
Tread gently, memories are here.
The sacrifice of children fatherless,
Of legless, armless, dying men of war.
Of laughing youths who laugh no more,
And horror heaped on horror wrought by war.
Was it for this that we have taken,
One lonely, desolate, dark despairing cross?
Nay! God has spoken.
One glorious empty cross,
One conquered tomb,
And spirit filled, one upper room
Answers man's long foreshadowed doom.
He knows his end shall be
Glorious Eternity.
Through mystic window sunlight streams,
Faint shadows, hopeful dreams.
Sunlight and all things fair,
Man's heritage is there.
Thine the Eternal Law;
Underpinning Peace, Overriding War.
Thy World, Thy War, Thy Word.
Thy body broken and Thy love out poured.
Before Thine Altar, Living Lord,
We bow the knee.
Our silence cries aloud, our need of Thee.

J.A.Dodsworth, 1981

****

"BEING DEAD YET SPEAKETH" ARMISTICE DAY 1924

****

We fought so long in touch with death,
That he became our Man of Rest.
And when he gave the word 'Fall Out.'
We stumbled, stricken, on his breast.
We did not think of Heaven nor Hell,
But, dying, wondered 'Is it well?'

Today the Dead rejoice 'Tis well,'
Britannias eyes still gleam with pride.
"My lands are free, we wear no chains,
We face the light." For this we died.
This was our gift. In all you give,
First thoughts, we plead, for those who live.

We fell and falling ceased to feel,
The scorching flame that round us played.
But some were left to carry on,
And we 'The Dead' implore full aid.
So when the 'Silence' is observed,
Think, have you done all we deserved?

George F. Martin, 10th November 1924

****

A SUMMER EVENING 1987

****

On a fine July night, without any fuss
At headquarters door stood a fine looking bus,
Stan was the driver, and Jimmy the boss -
Ev'ry one cheerful - no one was cross.

He stood at the door, clipboard in his hand,
and we set off down Tunnard street, feeling so grand,
We went through Carrington, Revesby - even saw some of the deer,
Saw the gardens and hedges, so pretty at this time of year.

Stan gave a good commentary, pointing out things as we rode,
He gave a good time to all of his load,
He showed us a mound, made me wonder if the owners were bent
for a Nuclear shelter for what is was meant!

In isolation it stood there in the evening light,
In the middle of a field no houses in sight,
If the button is pressed, and they want to feel safe
By gum, they wont half have to run at a hell of a pace!!

We saw Tennyson's Brook, rippling water and corn,
We went past the house where the poet was born,
We saw hundreds of cows, and sheep newly clipped -
the cows had been milked and the sheep had been dipped.

Then on through Sotby to Ulceby Cross,
Stan didn't seem at all at a loss,
He stopped at the local - a pub called 'The Gate'
Just to make sure we would not be late.

He then took us round for another good spin
and back to 'The Gate' - to shepherd us all in.
We all had a rest and another good drink
and by now the sun was beginning to sink.

Jimmy called us together and looked at the clock,
A departure signal for his precious flock,
We had enjoyed some good scenery all at the best,
But like crows at night - we come home to rest.

So back at headquarters, Vera opened the door,
We thought we were finished - but no there was more!
Our friends Nora and Vera had been busy as bees,
And had produced sandwiches, sausage rolls, coffee and teas.

This outing was given by the Boston Men's Branch,
To all of the Ladies - it was to give thanks,
But we thank the men - everyone and no less,
May you live long and prosper, as you help those in distress.

So from all the Ladies who had a good time
Our thanks to you all - in the words of the rhyme.

Ethel Taylor
President Ladies Section
Boston Branch of the Royal British Legion.

****

The time will come, when thou shalt lift thine eyes
To watch a long drawn battle in the skies,
While aged peasants, too amazed for words,
Stare at the flying fleets of wondrous birds.

England, so long the mistress of the sea,
Where winds and waves confess her sovereignty,
Her ancient triumphs yet on high shall bear,
And reign, the sovereign of the conquered air.

(from Luna Habitabilis - The Moon is inhabitable -

By Thomas Gray, 1738)

The Royal British Legion "ACT OF HOMAGE", is the middle verse of a poem by Laurence Binyon, here is the full poem.

FOR THE FALLEN

With proud thanksgiving, a mother for her children,
England mourns for her dead across the sea.
Flesh of her flesh they were, spirit of her spirit.
Fallen in the cause of the free.

Solemn the drums thrill; Death august and royal
Sings sorrow up into immortal spheres.
There is music in the midst of desolation
And glory that shines upon our tears.

They went with songs to the battle, they were young,
Straight of limb, true of eye, steady and aglow.
They were staunch to the end and against odds uncounted,
They fell with their faces to the foe.

They shall not grow old, as we that are left grow old;
Age shall not weary them, nor the years condemn.
At the going down of the sun and in the morning,
We will remember them.

They mingle not with their laughing comrades again;
They sit no more at familiar tables of home;
They have no lot in our labour of the day-time;
They sleep beyond England's foam.

But where desires are and our hopes profound,
Felt as a well-spring that is hidden from sight,
To the innermost heart of their own land they are known
As the stars are known to the night.

As the stars that shall be bright when we are dust,
Moving in marches upon the heavenly plain,
As the stars that are starry in the time of our darkness,
To the end, to the end they remain.

By Laurence Binyon.

BOSTON

This is of course Boston, Lincolnshire, and not the Boston over the water in Massachusetts, USA.

Apart from the five years I spent in the 1940's touring the British Isles and parts of Europe, all expenses paid! I have lived only a short hop-skip-and-a-jump from the picturesque town of Boston.

Kirton is my home which in the time of Elizabeth 1st was the third town of any size in the county of Lincolnshire. It even boasted a Grammar School where the famous Hansard of the House of Commons, was taught the Three R's

I digress, so back to Boston, which is not mentioned in the Doomsday Book, as was Kirton. But Boston grew with the railway and Dock traffic. Then in 1974 the Municipal Borough of Boston merged with the Boston Rural District creating a new area of 137 square miles with a population of some 52,000.

Highlights for the visitor include Market Days on Wednesday and Saturday each week. The Guildhall, Blackfriars Theatre, Sam Newsom Music Centre, Fydell House, Maud Foster Windmill. This is a five sail working Mill erected by Thomas and Isaac Recket in 1819.

Other buildings are the Assembly Rooms in the Market Place, Borough Council Buildings in West Street, Pescod Hall in Mitre Lane, Shodfriars Hall in South Street and, last but by no means least, St. Botolph's Church.

St. Botolph's Church is affectionately known by everyone as "Boston Stump". It is indeed a magnificent medieval lantern tower of Gothic design. Built in the years 1309 to 1520, it is one of the most beautiful lofty lantern towers in England, used during the war as a landmark for aircraft and I believe that it is used for the same purpose today.

The Statistics are of interest as follows:

	Feet	Metres
Total length	282	86

Total width	100	30.5
Length of nave	151	46
Height of tower to top of weather vanes	272	82.5
Width of tower	40	12
Length of the chancel	86	26
Width if chancel	30	9

Total area of church, more than 20,000 sq. ft. which means it is the largest parish church in England.

The tower contains a Ring of 10 bells, the largest weighing over one ton and tuned to a key of E flat. There is also a carillon of 15 bells and a faceless clock which chimes the quarters and tells the hours.

The following are unique to "The Stump"

365 steps to the Tower	Days in a year
52 windows	Weeks in a year
12 pillars	Months in a year
7 doors	Days in a week
24 steps to the library	Hours in a day
60 steps to the roof	Minutes in an hour
60 steps on each side of the Chancel	Seconds in a minute

More information can be found in "A TEN MINUTE GUIDE TO BOSTON PARISH CHURCH" compiled by John Orange 1978, also tours of the Church can be arranged by contacting The Stump Office, tel: 01205 362864.

Boston is rich in heritage and steeped in history, including the legacy of the Pilgrim Fathers. History tells us the Pilgrim Fathers tried to escape to Holland, but were betrayed and captured. Some of the leaders were detained in cells in the Guildhall, where you can sit in one of them today and ponder what were their thoughts as they awaited their fate. There is a Memorial to the Pilgrim Fathers standing on the bank of the River Witham in the Fishtoft area some 2 to 3 miles from the centre of Boston.

There is so much for the visitor to see in the Boston area, but also the resident is well catered for with various facilities.

The Geoff Moulder Leisure Pool provides all kinds of swimming facilities for the family. The Peter Paine Sports Centre provides facilities for roller-skating, badminton and bowls, whilst by Rochford Tower, there is ten pin bowling and squash.

Within a short distance from the town, both the visitor and resident will find ample space for fishing, walking, cycling, bird watching and golf.

There is something to suit everyone. Further detailed information can be obtained from Boston Borough Council, Municipal Buildings, West Street, Boston, Lincolnshire. PE21 8QR Tel: 01205 357400.

BOSTON has a firm link with America. This takes us back to The Pilgrim Fathers, who were the most famous of the early colonists who had strong connections with Boston and surrounding areas. The ship named "MAYFLOWER" carried the Pilgrim Fathers to North America in 1620. One of the notable names being Rev. John Cotten who resigned his living as the vicar of St. Botolphs - "The Stump", hence the Cotten Chapel carries his name.

BOSTON also has a strong connection with Australia, as I do also. My son, Keith, has been a resident around Sydney in the Blue Mountain area for the past 24 years. He is a member of the RAFA and his story on a touring holiday later in this book makes very interesting reading, and, no doubt, makes many of us envious!

Getting back to the connection between Boston and "Down-Under". There are many famous names that make this connection including:

Sir Joseph Banks, squire of Revesby and the Recorder and Freeman of Boston, sailed with Captain Cook on the ship H.M.S. Endeavour.

Incidentally, there is a replica of ENDEAVOUR that was launched on the 9th December 1993, and commissioned in April 1994. It has been circumnavigating Australia and I saw it in Sydney Harbour in January 1995. Cook sailed with upwards of 90 people on board, how they survived such cramped conditions is a mystery, perhaps even a miracle, the replica has a crew of around 40.

Famous names: George Bass, a native from near sleaford, his family later moved to Boston, discovered Bass Strait, between Australia and Tasmania. Captain Matthew Flinders, a native from Donington, with a road in Boston carrying his name, together with George Bass, named a number of places after names from around Boston. Bicker Island, Sleaford Island, Boston Island and I believe there are more. Joseph Gilbert was another Bostonian on Cook's expedition, from which the Gilbert Islands derived their name.

The Guildhall is a good source of further information, open to visitors throughout the year. Tel: 01205 365954.

Stanley Naylor.

BOSTON

The Grand Sluice gates on the River Witham, keeps the salt water from flowing into the fresh water, was opened in 1766 and a banquet was held to celebrate the occasion. Just because a certain disgruntled London reporter was not invited, he is alleged to have written the following verse:

> Boston, Boston, what hast thou to boast on,
> Save a Grand Sluice and a Tall Steeple,
> A proud, conceited, ignorant people,
> And a coast where souls get lost on.

***

BOSTON STUMP

Dr. William Stukely wrote the following verse when visiting Boston in 1707.

> "Across the Washes ... stands Boston ... Tis remarkable for its beautiful Church and Steeple which is reckoned the highest tower in Europe: Saluting travellers at a great distance round, and an excellent Seamark seen about 40 miles distant. All the Country tao' there are very fine Churches ... but this one looks them all like a proud Dame sensible of her beauty and scorning the meaner Crowd about her".

THE PILGRIM FATHERS MEMORIAL FISHTOFT, BOSTON,

Erected 1957.

Written at the base is this verse:

> "Near this place in September 1607 those later known as the Pilgrim Fathers set sail on their first attempt to find religious freedom across the seas"

Discovering New Lands
by Keith Naylor

It was a fine afternoon as with a mighty thrust the jet taxied along the runway out into Botany Bay, then, pointing its nose into the clear blue sky, headed towards the clouds and the silent world above. With only two refuelling stops at Singapore and Muscat (Arabian Sea), it didn't seem long before I was walking into the terminal of London's Heathrow Airport, one of the busiest in the world.

I was met by my father, and we set off on our four-hour drive back to my home county of Lincolnshire, along some of the fairly fast motorways of England. My home village of Kirton is central for the county, in flat but fertile reclaimed fenland, dissected by many drainage dykes. It is the stronghold of the tulip and daffodil growing industry. Production is so good that bulbs are being exported to Holland.

I would like to mention all my many drives through the beautiful spring countryside, but two of my favourites I must describe as to me they are the true England, which millions of tourists seek every year.

The first excursion was in the company of my mother, heading towards north-west England, passing by Chesterfield, one of the hubs of industrial England. Our first stop for a few days was Manchester, to visit relatives. This city has a face that is constantly changing, slums being demolished to be replaced by concrete structures.

Leaving Manchester via the M6 motorway it was only a couple of hours before we were entering the town of Kendal, the gateway to the picturesque Lake District, the land of granite and slate-built homes and dry-stone walls on every horizon. It was the height of spring in Cumbria; and in Ambleside, a gorgeous lakeside village, everything was in full bloom all over the many rock gardens. Seeing daffodils reminded me that this was one of the homes of William Wordsworth and one of his many famous lines: "A host, of golden daffodils". We found accommodation at the town of Keswick and as it was still very light we went for an evening drive into the mountains through the beautifully named villages of Thurlmere, Buttermere and Threlkeld, where everything was so peaceful. We watched the sun sending its last blaze of light over the mountains before it seemingly hid behind the highest peak for the night. The following morning brought the crisp mountain air, the song of the chaffinch, and the sight of ducks skimming the calm, reflective lake of Derwent water. A stroll along its shoreline in the warm morning sun gave you the feeling of a long searched-for tranquillity.

Sadly, we left the Lake District, crossing the Pennine range of mountains, through the Yorkshire moors to our last stop before home, the city of York, one of the oldest, and best preserved walled cities in Europe.

My other favourite area of England is the beautiful, historical, and unspoiled Cotswolds, comprising two counties, Gloucestershire and Oxfordshire with quaint villages such as Bourton-on-the-Water, Upper Slaughter, Lower Slaughter, Chipping Campden and Broadway. The houses here are built of the golden honey-coloured limestone. The unique domestic architecture of the villages moulds itself into the rolling, rich green landscape. Dry-stone walling has been a lingering art in the Cotswolds for centuries, replacing the hedges which neighbouring counties possess. The River Windrush winds its way through villages, the sun glistening on its slow-flowing, shallow waters, edged with lush grass, draped by weeping willows; such a relaxing scene is so hard to drive away from.

Now comes the longest drive of my holidays. With my parents, I drove from England, through France to our destination of Madrid, Spain, to visit relatives I hadn't seen for more than 10 years. Taking the one-and-a-half hours' ferry ride across the Channel from Dover to Calais, we had a full day's drive ahead of us to our night stop at Angouleme.

Driving on the right hand side of the road with a right-hand drive car wasn't too hard to get used to, but overtaking was a totally new experience. The driver is driving blind when coming up behind a vehicle, so it is up to the passenger to see if the road is clear. Slowly edging out, you see this truck bearing down on you from the other direction; you practically jump into the driver's lap to make sure you're as far on the right side of the road as possible. French roads are fast and straight, avenued by a variety of trees, making it a pleasure to drive along them. Everywhere the fruit trees were in blossom; it was a pity we didn't have more time to stop and take in the prettiness of the sunny countryside.

Morning brought an early continental breakfast, and the headache of the one way system of Angouleme. Following signposted roads we were soon on our way. Once we had passed through the sprawling city of Bordeaux, all that was left was the French-Spanish border then, meeting no international problems, we were in Spain.

The first stop was for petrol. The attendant came out to fill up the car with this highly priced commodity. Trying to make conversation, we asked if she spoke English. There was a quick answer "no". In very broken English, the attendant asked if we spoke Spanish; naturally the answer was "no", so that was the abrupt end of the conversation. The scenery completely changed, once we had negotiated the Pyrenees, to land tilled to infertility, no trees, dryness; and the most obvious sight in each town we passed through was poverty, something I had never experienced before. Using the many new tollways we soon entered the heart of Spain, Madrid, where the weather is mild all the year round, the parks so green, and fountains so varied and spectacular. Aided by our relatives, we visited such attractions as the Plaza Mayor, Puerta del Sol where Ernest Hemmingway stayed while writing his famed novel "Death in the Afternoon", the Rastro, Madrid's flea market, and Plaza de Espana. The most impressive visit was to the Royal Palace, a building of five storeys and 2500 rooms; it took three hours to walk through 50 rooms, each rooms individually ornamented with gold or silver.

One day was spent over the mountains in the province of Segovia, the land of medieval castles, and in the town of Segovia, visiting the most genuine Spanish castle, or Alcazar, which was romantically impressive, a structure of Moorish design yet looking as though it should have been in Bavaria.

The most memorable event was an evening at the Corrida de Toros in the Madrid Bullring. Luckily it was the middle of the St Isidro celebrations, the bullfight festival of Madrid, so we were able to see some master matadors. After an opening grand parade of alguacillos, matadors, banderilleros, picadors and cuadrillas, the first of six bulls comes into the ring to meet his fate. If you concentrate on the matador and not on the torture of the bull, you begin to appreciate this Spanish art, and understand what the roars and the tremors of the crowd are for. Straight after the bull-fight, it was off to a restaurant for a traditional meal of lamb and sangria, a traditional bar wine, flamenco dancing and guitar music. This marked the end of our holiday, so going back via the route we came, it was "adios" to Madrid.

Back in England, it wasn't long before it was time to pack my bags once again, and with a sad and final farewell to my parents at Heathrow Airport, I boarded my plane for Toronto, Canada. The city of Toronto is the cleanest and most modern I have ever seen, well planned with the historical buildings retained, blending in with the modern complexes. Having only half a day before flying out, I took a bus tour of the city, seeing such sights at Parliament Buildings, Casa Loma, New City Hall, downtown Toronto, the Toronto Islands and, lastly, the University campus, which is spread over a wide area - it could be up to half a mile between one lesson and the next so there are some of the fittest students in the world here.

Taking an Air Canada flight in the afternoon down to Windsor, I was met by relatives who live in the towns of Leamington and Kingsville, which are the tomato and tobacco capitals of Canada. While in the area, I took the opportunity to see the magnificent Niagara Falls, where the noise is deafening, and you can see the spray rising about 500 feet up, from the force of the falls. There is an exhilarating but expensive way of having a shower here, by taking a ride on the boat, Maid of the Mist, which takes you into the spray at the bottom of the falls.

Flying back to Toronto to catch the Canadian Pacific train across to Calgary, I had time before boarding the train to go up the CN Tower, a communications aid which is the tallest freestanding structure in the world at about 553m or 1815ft. The glorious view from the tower is worth anybody's time. Back to earth, and all aboard for my two-days' train ride through great pine forests, around lakes and across the plains of Manitoba and Saskatchewan, to Calgary, Alberta. While you are having dinner, a steward re-arranges the carriage to individual berths with curtains all set up. It reminded me of the "Murder on the Orient Express" story; I was certainly hoping the events of that story didn't happen on this train.

Leaving Calgary where oil and the Calgary Stampede have brought prosperity to the province, I joined a bus tour which was to take me all the way through the Rockies to Vancouver, making stops at Banff, Lake Louise, Jasper and Kamloops. I was unable to see the Rockies the first day because a shower had brought in low cloud, but on the second day the sun broke through, revealing the awe-inspiring snow-capped Rocky Mountains looming above the Trans-Canadian Highway. I believe this is how everybody should have their first sight of the Rockies, as it seems to make them much more breathtaking.

The beauty of these mountains has to be seen to be believed. Lake Louise was the most enjoyable place of the tour, a perfect fairytale setting, a glacier-fed lake, mirroring the surrounding mountains, pine forests and shimmering waterfalls in its crystal-clear but icy water. Standing at the end of Lake Louise, a hotel that could make you believe you were in Bavaria, Austria or Switzerland, but no, it's the Canadian Rockies where such fairytales are possible. A wide variety of wildlife can be sighted, mule deer, rocky mountain goats, black bear, chipmunks and marmots.

After a Western Airlines Aloha flight from Vancouver to Honolulu, yet another paradise was introduced to me. The hotel overlooked Waikiki Beach, so the first thing to do was to have a swim in the warm turquoise sea. I had only one-and-a-half days' stopover here so, on the advice of a local travel agent, I took a full day's tour of Oahu. This is the island Honolulu is situated on, the third largest island of the Hawaiian group, where 92 per cent of the island's population live in Honolulu. The tour followed the coast road, revealing colossal volcanic rock formations. The first long stop was at Hanauma Bay, a marine park where I was able to go snorkelling among shoals of vari-coloured fish. The guide pointed out many aptly named rock formations, such as Diamond Head, Lions Head and the Rabbit. Kahuku Beach was the remote lunch stop, lunch consisting of a variety of fruits to satisfy individual tastes. The return journey was through the centre of the tow ranges of mountains of Oahu where pineapple plantations flourish. Back in Honolulu, all that was left to do was pack my bags again for my midnight flight back to Sydney, and sadly the end of a tremendous holiday.

KEITH NAYLOR

The Mail Train

Some time ago we were reminiscing about the railway journeys made while we were in the RAF. Those who lived in Boston at the time will recall coming home on leave and forty-eights via Peterborough - nearly always on the "Mail Train".

This usually meant that you had managed to get to Peterborough from the far ends of the country only to find that the last train of the evening for Boston had left and you had to wait for the first one of the next day. The carriages would be standing cold and empty in the blacked-out station, waiting for the train from London with the day's newspapers and mail for Spalding, Boston, North Lincs and Grimsby.

On being coupled to an engine the train became dimly lit, though never really warmed. Gradually more bods would arrive and occupy the vacant seats until all the compartments were full and eventually in the early hours of the morning the train left Peterborough North heading for home but stopping at every wayside station.

Many will have memories of the Mail Train - like the matelot whose ship was just home from a tour in the Pacific; he neglected to tell anyone he wanted to get off at Boston and woke in a siding at Cleethorpes!

The journey I recall most on the Mail Train was really rather sad - as the compartment filled up we talked and discovered who our travelling companions were. I remember some of them - like the sailor going to join a minesweeper at Grimsby, an Army bod coming home on leave like myself, and a RAF Corporal returning from leave to Coningsby.

Eventually the shadowy figure on the platform blew his whistle and swung his lamp and the train started to move. At the last minute a breathless girl in civvies jumped into our compartment and squeezed into the space of the seat next to the Corporal. As the carriage lights brightened we could make out that she would have appeared quite pretty if she had been in smarter clothes and not looking so tired-eyed.

I assumed that she might have just finished a shift in a factory from her appearance and the fact that she soon dropped off to sleep, with her head on the Corporal's shoulder. After a few minutes she became quite restless and started mumbling in her sleep - "We must get another forty made this week - beat the target - another forty more -"

Gradually she became quiet, but remained still with her head on his shoulder, and we resumed our previous talk which had turned to the subject of air raids on our cities. This had set off the Corporal, who was going into gory detail of the mayhem of one particular direct hit on one of the London street markets, where there were many civilian casualties.

As he was carrying on at great length the girl started gently sobbing, although she still appeared to be asleep. He was continuing with his story and seemed to relish describing the disaster when she suddenly shot up out of the seat with a cry and stumbled out into the corridor - "My Mother and Father were killed in that raid!"

She didn't come back and nobody talked much after that, least of all the Corporal.

JIM JACKSON RAFA

The late Adrian Thorpe was a member of the Boston Branch RAFA committee and gave me a number of reports he had prepared for the station magazine when he was STATION HEALTH & SAFETY OFFICER at RAF Coningsby. Prior to being SHSO, Adrian had had a long career in the Royal Air Force.

These three reports have been chosen for inclusion in this book, because we can all relate to them. But also they have been chosen as a tribute to Adrian and in memory of a lovely man whom I was privileged to know. He was held in esteem and great affection by his fellow committee members. To a great man!

S.N.

Why is it that?

Why is it that when I am driving about the station observing the speed limit, being a conscientious member of the Road Safety Committee, that I often get tailgated by people who would really rather overtake me?

Why is it that as I drive between my home in Boston and work at Coningsby I sometimes have to pick my way through great clods of soil dropped from farming and contractors' vehicles?

Why is it that so often when I am driving along the Queen's highway I see rubbish being hurled out of the window of the vehicle in front?

Why is it that when I walk through Boston on a Saturday afternoon my senses are assaulted by the sheer coarseness and vulgarity of many of the young people who congregate there? And why do so many of them smoke?

Why is it that so many cyclists choose not to carry lights at night?

Why is it that people walking their dogs at night take on the same coloration as their companions, which are almost invariably black?

Why is it that when I pull up at traffic lights, the leviathan (truck) behind me comes to within what seems to me to be a millimetre of my rear bumper?

Why is it that when they lower the water level in the Maud Foster Drain in Boston you find out where a lot of the supermarket trolleys finish up?

Why is it that some drivers dazzle me with their bright red fog lights on a gin-clear night?

Why is it that people leaving the Castle Club make a point of leaving a few items of glassware around the place, broken or otherwise?

Why is it that the foot-scraper grating that used to be at the front entrance to the Castle Club has been carefully folded in half and cast aside?

Why is it that when you see something awful going on, like the three card trick being pulled on a tourist, or bad public behaviour of any other kind, there isn't a policeman within miles?

Why is it that on one page of my daily paper they will bleat about the exploitation of women, and on the next page they carry an advert for ladies' undies being worn scantily and provocatively by a gorgeous girl - sorry - woman?

Why is it that when one huge truck is inching slowly past another one on a dual carriage-way, the one being overtaken will never ease off a touch so that the manoeuvre can be completed more quickly?

Why is it that cyclists don't believe that one way signs apply to them? Why is it that no matter how clearly you mark an official car parking slot, somebody without authority will use it, and it is generally mine?

Adrian Thorpe.

NICOTIANA TABACUM

I suppose you have guesses that the title to this piece is the Latin name for tobacco. For your further enlightenment it belongs to the family Solanaceae, which translates as the Nightshade family. No wonder some people think that tobacco is poisonous.

You may recall that in my January article I invited you to ring in if you wanted me to write about smoking. It transpires that the 13th March is to be National No Smoking Day, so the March Number would seem to be a good one for the topic. Unfortunately, the window between the appearance of the January Interceptor and the deadline for March copy was a bit narrow, so it's coming, ready or not. In any case, so many people keep asking me about smoking and its avoidance that this might help me get a bit of peace. There is further evidence about interest in the subject in the rate at which those little "No Smoking" symbols keep disappearing from the Health and Safety display in the Education Centre. I have got rid of literally hundreds.

My own history as a smoker is not particularly commendable. When I was a young and impoverished Aircraft Apprentice in the early fifties my Dad had a shop, and in my regular food parcels would appear consignments of unpopular brands of cigarettes well past their sell-by date. Mind you, in those days smoking wasn't bad for you. The old boys that used to get their fags from my Dad used to cough and rumble a lot until they got their old age pensions and then die of consumption, pneumonia, Rising of the Lights or some other medieval complaint. Lung cancer hadn't been invented. To continue my chequered career, after one memorable night out in Cyprus in the early sixties I felt so ill that I didn't light up again for two years. Just to finish off this sad tale, my wife and I as non-smokers at the time, took a holiday in Torquay. We socialised with a pair of smokers and decided to join them in their fug for the week. It took us both another eighteen months to stop again.

Some of what I have said brings me to the position of smokers. I have a deep sympathy for people who are addicted. Let there be no doubt about it; in the vast majority of cases those who smoke have virtually no choice in the matter. Once a certain amount of time has passed since the last gasper, body points out to brain that its nicotine level is dropping to an unacceptably low level, and will it further ensure that a bit more dried leaf of a variety of the Nightshade family is ignited a bit smartish and the results of said combustion pulled into the lungs without undue delay, otherwise it is going to get cross. I don't know if the organisation called FOREST (Freedom Organisation for the Right to Enjoy Smoking Tobacco) still exists, but if it does I am sorry. Freedom doesn't come into it. The word should be compulsion. FOREST used to have a very famous patron of RAF origin. I hope he has left.

Let me tell you of the harm smoking has done from my own experience:

Eight years ago my wife and I watched her father die of lung cancer. We haven't smoked since.

When I worked for Short Bros our Supply Controller started having trouble getting round the golf course because his legs hurt. The specialist said: "Tom, if you continue to smoke, and I don't treat your condition, you will probably lose a leg. And if you don't stop smoking, I'm not going to treat you". Tom stopped. Fear is a great motivator.

My son had an ulcer; pressure of work and all that. The doctor said that smoke was aggravating his condition. He stopped, and is now becoming quite agreeable company again.

I don't intend to go into detail of what tobacco smoke can do. You will all probably have seen the findings about the effects of passive smoking, and the deterioration that smoking mothers can cause in foetuses. There is plenty of publicity and advice available on the subject, and I have got loads of it. If you want some please get in touch, or raid the display in the Education Centre. MOD policy on smoking is in JSP 375, Volume 2, Leaflet 3. By the way, I wonder what contribution smoking makes to the greenhouse effect?

Adrian Thorpe

LAUGHTER

I expect that by now you will have forgotten the article that appeared in the press early in September about laughter being good for the health. It seems that laughter sets off the old creative stuff among your bodily thingies to produce killer cells for the destruction of nasties. No less an authority than The Reader's Digest has a regular feature which proclaims that laughter is the best medicine.

Naturally the Ministry of Defence seized on this and produced a policy document with some very interesting recommendations. Some of them are reproduced here for your consideration:

Tickling sticks are available from Supply and Movements Squadrons, either by local purchase or under an appropriate Management Code.

Chuckle muscle exercise programmes will be set up by Physical Education Flights.

The Les Dennis Laughter Show is to be required viewing for officers feeling gloomy after their latest phase check results from the Individual Studies School.

Education Centres will distribute free tickets to Doddy's new show at the London Palladium, if it's still running by the time you read this.

Along with the positive items such as those above, there are some warnings for the incautious:

Laughing till you're fit to bust is considered to be dangerous.

Laughing till you cry is not felt to be in the best traditions of the Service (female personnel may exercise discretion in this matter).

Now that I have got your attention, or even if I haven't, those of you who are quite elderly will remember an old saying from way back. It described what was generally required of erks in their day-to-day avoidance of trouble. It went something like: "If it moves, salute it; if it's on the ground, pick it up; if you can't pick it up, paint it". Things aren't quite like that any more, but if you do happen to see the odd thing lying about making the place look untidy, please pick it up and put it in the nearest bin. It might make the world a little safer.

Adrian Thorpe

Lincolnshire Aircraft Recovery Group

The night of the eighth of May 1941 was a very bright moonlit night. Pilot Officer D.W. Thompson with P/O Britain as his A1 operator were ordered out on patrol from RAF Wittering at 23:35 hrs. They took off in a Beaufighter I of 25 sqd A Flight. They were vectored South of Digby. At 14,000 ft and north of the wash they picked up a bleep on their radar. They set chase, which lasted for about three minutes. In front of them and slightly below, some 400 yards away, at approximately 13,000 feet, the silhouette of an enemy aircraft could be seen. It stood out stark and clear in the bright moonlight on the cloud layer some 6,000 ft below them. Both P/O Thompson and P/O Britain agreed that it was a Dornier 215. The aircraft, in fact, was a Dornier 17 ZK 10, an early night fighter one of only ten built.

P/O Thompson realised he was approaching the enemy too fast so he throttled back causing flames to appear from the engines exhausts. Although up-moon of the enemy aircraft the approaching Beaufighter had been seen and as P/O Thompson fired a one second burst of tracer the German managed to avoid them.

The three crew on board the Dornier that night were Pilot F.W. Wilheim Lettermeier, his wireless operator Unft Georg Herden and Uffz Herbert Thomas. Lettermeier was on his first nightfighter combat mission. Herbert Thomas, a more experienced flier, with about 40 missions to his credit, since July 1940, had been assigned the task of training the young Pilots on their first few trips. They were all from the 2/NJG 2 nightfighter sqd from Gilze Rijen. The aircraft, a Dornier 17 ZK 10, a conversion from the DO 17 bomber, and fitted with the early Liechtenstein radar and cannon, coded R4+GK and Wrk No 2843.

After avoiding the first attack by a steep turn to port, the pilot, thinking he had lost the Beaufighter, returned to a straight course again, unaware that P/O Thompson's Beaufighter had picked them up again and was closing in for the kill. Thompson, now only a hundred yards away, fired a short burst from below and to starboard. The first burst caught the starboard engine and with the Dornier diving to port the port engine was then hit. The engine immediately burst into flames and the aircraft started to spiral down. Inside the Dornier the crew had all been slightly injured by flying splinters but were still able to carry out practised procedure taken in such an event:- ignition out, petrol cock off and full throttle to clear the remaining petrol in the pipes. Lettermeier and Thomas pulled hard on the control column but were unable to correct the spiral dive. Herbert Thomas gave the order to bail out. He saw Georg Herden jettison his cover.

What happened during the next few seconds was very vague, as Thomas recalled. As he felt a terrific knock and his senses became dimmed, he was aware of the heat all around him. He felt a lot of pain. Suddenly everything went quiet until the pain shot through him again. All seemed as if he had been drugged. He believes that with the canopy gone he was dragged out of the aircraft by suction and was thrown against the tailplane. His parachute harness may have caught some part of the tail as the straps were found to be slightly torn afterwards. Without realising it, he must have pulled the rip-cord and the opening chute must have dragged him clear from the falling aircraft.

Where, and how long, he had been lying on the ground he did not know. When he regained consciousness he believed he was in heaven because his parachute had covered him completely and the bright moonlight shining through the chute gave him this impression. He then heard voices which seemed very distant. People started to arrive and stand around him. Someone may have pushed a Woodbine between his lips. He soon found himself sat in a car with Georg Herden next to him. They were in the charge of the local constable P.C. Cutts. They were told that Lettermeier had not survived the crash. In fact, he had bailed out but the Dornier was too low and he was found about 100 yds from the crash site.

Thomas next remembered waking up on the operating table and being very embarrassed as a young nurse cut off his flying suit and uniform. After he came out of the anaesthetic he found himself encased in plaster. Beside him sat a heavily armed soldier. The soldier later became a good friend, especially because of his Woodbines, which he generously shared with Thomas. The friendship was soon to end, as escape was impossible, the guard was assigned to other duties. Herbert Thomas received quite good treatment in the hospital being cursed as the 'damned German pilot' by the doctors and nurses. He was in a ward hidden by a screen around his bed. One

Sunday the screen was removed, making him the talking point of the hospital visitors. He remembers a little boy placing a toffee on his bed covers. After two or three months he was moved to No. 4 Military Hospital in Knutsford, Cheshire. He was eventually repatriated to Germany as his injuries were considered too severe to let him take any active part in the war.

Forty-three years after this event the Lincolnshire Aircraft Recovery Group located the final resting place of Herbert Thomas's rare Dornier 17 ZK 10 aircraft. After obtaining the relevant permissions from the M.O.D. and the land owners, the L.A.R.G. set about recovering the remains of the aircraft. A preliminary search of the site with metal detectors proved fruitless with only a few fragments of metal being found.

This was later found to be due to the fact the aircraft had crashed onto a riverbank which had in later years been levelled off, so removing any surface wreckage that may have been there.

It was on an August morning in 1984 that the L.A.R.G. turned up on site armed with a Hymac and started the recovery.

At a depth of about 15ft the first signs of the aircraft were found as Glycol and oil seeped into the hole. Amongst the first large pieces of wreckage to come out was the complete and intact tail wheel tyre and tube. The tube was later taken to a local garage and inflated and has remained inflated ever since. As the dig continued vast amounts of wreckage were uncovered. At a final depth of approximately 35 ft part of the reduction gear was pulled out. Amongst the items recovered were approximately one third of one of the Bramo Fafnir engines, two MG 17 machine guns, a badly torn dingy and survival kit, complete with flare pistol and flares. Also found in the wreckage was a briefcase which belonged to Georg Herden. It included the navigational maps and code books, his 'kappi' (forage cap) and his handkerchief with his initials on it.

In April 1986 L.A.R.G. group members met Herbert Thomas at the Hendon Aircraft Museum, London, where they presented him with some pieces of his Dornier, including the ignition keys.

On the 17th. July 1987 a unique occasion took place at RAF Coningsby, when two World War II combatants met again, just 46 years after they first met over the skies of Lincolnshire.

Herbert Thomas, now 64 years of age, a German airman returned to England to collect some more of the remains of his Dornier DO 17Z K10 nightfighter aircraft, which had been recovered by L.A.R.G. in 1984.

To present the wreckage to him was the man that shot him down back in 1941, then P.O. Dennis Britain, now aged 85 years.

The presentation was arranged by the Lincolnshire Aircraft Recovery Group and Royal Air Force Coningsby. They were hosts to some 50 people, including 16 wartime German Airmen from the Association of Former Nightfighter Groups, Mr Castle-Miller a wartime Intelligence Officer from 25 Squadron, Mr. 'Rick' Pilchar, the surgeon who operated on Herr Thomas, and Mr. Sargent, son of the Home Guard who first captured Herr Thomas.

A tour of RAF Coningsby was organised, and the German Air Force arranged for a Dornier 28 to collect the Dornier DO 17 wreckage, which was escorted by two Phantom Jets.

by David Stubley. L.A.R.G.

ALBEMARLE V 1610

The researching of aircraft crashes can take a long time, years in fact, one example of this was the recovery of Armstrong Whitworth Albemarle V 1910, done by the Lincolnshire Aircraft Recovery Group.

From the time the group was first formed there had been rumours of an Albemarle that had crashed during the war, at Kirton Fen, between Boston and Coningsby. In 1986 the site was located, from the evidence of small wreckage on the field and a good reading given by metal detectors, indicating deeper wreckage. Ministry of Defence permission to recover had to be gained, this proved to be the first hold up.

To obtain permission the aircraft make, serial number and date of crash must be quoted. After talking with locals various rumours concerning the identity and circumstances of the crash came to light, "the aircraft had been shot down by RAF Coningsby defenses" "it had been shot down by a Beaufighter" "the recovery crew had said it was a three engined prototype". Dates varied from 1940 to 45, most said it was an Albemarle, a few said it was a Blenheim.

With all Albemarles researched from known records, no aircraft showed itself to be our aircraft. A Blenheim, according to records, had crashed 3 miles SW of Tattershall, this location showed possibilities. MOD permission was applied for and duly granted.

It was now August 1988, the crop had been harvested over the site, a mechanical digger had been arranged for, this, however was not available until the 2nd week. We decided to do a preliminary dig with spades, the weekend before to clear any wreckage which lay near the surface, so saving time when the digger arrived the next weekend.

The first find was a propeller blade, digging down deeper, we were disappointed not to find an engine. Our attention was soon drawn to what appeared to be a cylinder some 30 inches long and 8 inches in diameter. Though we did not think it was a bomb, we were not sure what it could be.

Being wary of other ordnance like photo-flashes etc. a decision was made to contact the EOD via the local police, as regulations state. To our surprise a REME Unit attended coming from Chatham, Kent, passing the RAF EOD Unit at Wittering on the way to the site.

Not knowing what the cylinder was, the engineers prepared to blow the cylinder open by controlled explosion. As the site was in a very dry cornfield the Fire Brigade were asked to attend, amidst blue flashing lights at 11pm in the evening, the charge was detonated. All this to find that the cylinder contained a black fluid, probably hydraulic fluid. The site was declared safe and digging would be allowed to continue.

With the attendance of the digger, the full excavation proved to be a bit of an anti-climax compared with the previous weeks excitement, the hoped for two engines not being found. Items recovered showed extensive signs of fire damage and included several shattered engine cylinders and parts from the fuselage, but no positive proof of identification. One major item recovered in good condition was a propeller boss at a depth of 7 ft.

On inspection of the engine parts and the prop. boss, it was clear to see that they were not from a Blenheim aircraft. The cylinders were of sleeve valve type, as fitted to the Albemarle.

At the dig was one of the locals he added more information by saying that one of those killed was called Tom Whittome from Peterborough and that the aircraft had come from a Derby Airfield. We quickly consulted our research notes accumulated over the research period. A brief mention of an Albemarle in Simon Parrys 'Intruders Over Britain' shot down by German Night-Fighter may have been the aircraft, as one of the crew killed was an A.A. Whittome. However according to the book the Albemarle was lost near Great Yarmouth. Was Albemarle V 1610 the aircraft we had recovered, consultation with the MOD informing them of the facts soon proved it to be the case.

V 1610 from 42 OTU was shot down on 23rd April 1944 whilst on a night cross country flying exercise. It had flown from RAF Ashbourne in Derbyshire. The crew consisted of:- Sgt J.E. Hutchinson, Pilot. Sgt K. Rusby, Navigator; Sgt. A.A. Whittome, Bomb Aimer. These three were all killed. The two survivors were: Sgt J. Davis, Wireless Operator and Sgt R.W. Thurgood, Air Gunner.

On further research, Sgt Davis had told his story in a book on RAF Ashbourne by Malcolm Giddings, unfortunately he could not be relocated to reunite him with parts of his aircraft. Sgt Thurgood also could not be found, it is believed he has moved away to Australia.

For the next 4 years, research continued on V 1610 but with little success. Author and researcher Ian McLachlan had been interested in V 1610, as it was shot down on the same night as the American 8th Airforce had mounted a major offensive, a subject he was researching. Ian had made an appeal to locate relatives or friends of any of the crew who were on the Albemarle. By good fortune, Mr Kenneth F Rusby, son of the navigator, had responded to the appeal. Mr Rusby had been researching his fathers flying career for the last 20 years, but was not aware that the aircraft had been recovered or in fact, where it had crashed.

Ken was able to furnish the LARG with a lot more information and photographs about the incident involving his father. Consequently we were able to complete a more comprehensive display.

On the 25th April 1992 Ken Rusby, with his mother, Mrs J.G. Laycock (formerly Mrs J.G. Rusby) and his family attended a memorial service at the Lincolnshire Aviation Heritage Centre. Here a plaque was unveiled in memory of his father and the rest of the crew killed in Albermarle V 1610

By David Stubley L.A.R.G.

THE TRAGEDY OF WAR

I became involved in this story when I attended a reunion of 83 Squadron at RAF Coningsby on Saturday 7th May 1983 and a Service in Coningsby Church on Sunday 8th. May 1983.

As the story unfolded during the weekend, I gleaned a lot of material, and also I am indebted to Ron Low, Reunion Secretary to 83, Squadron, for his contribution.

The story revolves around three Lancaster Pilots and a Dutch Flag, but one should start at the beginning.

Two of the pilots were Australian and a Canadian, the third was a British Pilot, Flight Lieut. Ronald Walker, whose home was in Wigan, but was stationed at RAF Coningsby with 83, (Pathfinder) Squadron at the time of this event.

The crew of Lancaster No. V ND551 were:

Pilot & Captain	Flight Lieut. R.A. Walker D.F.C.
Navigator	Flight Lieut. N.J. Cornell
Bomb Aimer	Flight Lieut. J.R. Wells
Engineer	Flight Serg. H.E. Holdersworth
Wireless Operator	Flight Serg. R.C. Bailey
Rear Gunner	Flight Serg. D.R. Kelly
Mid Upper Gunner	Flight Serg. C.R. Taylor

I believe that all the crew had medals, but I do not have the correct information.

On the night of 21st/22nd. June 1944 Lancaster V ND551 departed from RAF Coningsby, the mission being to mark and bomb the town of Wesseling, which lies about 9 miles south of Cologne in Germany. This was the crews 46th operational flight over enemy territory, from which they failed to return.

Nothing was heard of the fate of the aircraft and crew until the 3rd. November 1944, when a letter was received from the Red Cross Society with the information that six members of the crew had lost their lives, but the question for families of the 7 man crew, which one was missing and where was he? A further report stated that the Lancaster had been shot down by a German Night Fighter some ten miles south of Eindhoven.

The one that survived was Flight Lieut. Ronald Walker, and he arrived at a farm belonging to a Mr. J. Verhoven (I have been told the farmer's name was Jaques Martens, so I'm not sure which one is correct). The farmer's wife thought it was a German, but a Dutch resistance worker confirmed the airman was British. It is worth noting that the farmer's daughter was already in a German prison for helping British Pilots, so the situation was not comfortable for all parties concerned.

Ronald Walker had been slightly injured in his fall from the aircraft, but had already walked about three miles heading for the Belgian border. It was not safe to move any further dressed in a British uniform, so Ronald Walker was hidden in a cornfield.

That evening Ronald changed into some Dutch clothing and with the aid of Walter De Vries cycled 12/13 miles to the village of Nuenan. He was then safely conducted to another farm at Wettens, where he stayed for a week. Ronald even helped on the farm and a 15 year old girl from a neighbouring farm tried teaching him the Dutch language.

Unknown to Ronald of course he was really being honoured in England. On the 27th. June 1944 he was awarded the D.F.C. - Distinguished Flying Cross for his unstinting and outstanding war service.

At the farm owned by Petrus J. Kuyten, Ronald Walker met with Flying Officer Jack Nott, an Australian Pilot. Then on the evening of the 29th. June, Walter De Vries and two other Dutch resistance men escorted the two Pilots to another village. Narrowly missing being stopped by a German patrol, the two Pilots arrived at the home of France van Dijk in Waaire, where they met two Canadians.

All four were then moved to the home of the van Moorsel sisters in Waalre, where they stayed for about a week. At first the atmosphere was a bit tense, but soon they were chatting and singing late into the evenings.

It was on the 8th. July that the opportunity came to move the four airmen to Tilburg in order to make contact with the Belgian underground movement. Each of them being supplied with false Dutch and Belgian passports.

At 8.00 o'clock that evening the car set out with Ronald Walker and Jack Nott arriving safely at the home of "Aunt Coba", 49, Dispenstraat, Tilburg. "Aunt Coba", her real name being Jacoba Pulskens, was an ageing spinster who had defied the Germans in hiding other airmen and Jews in her home. It was here at "Aunt Coba's" that Ronald and Jack met with another Canadian Pilot, Flying Officer Roy Carter.

Having delivered the two airmen safely at "Aunt Coba's", the car returned to Waalre to pick up the remaining two Canadians. Unfortunately on the journey back to Tilburg the car was stopped by a German patrol of six. The occupants of the car were stripped and the false passports, escape material, maps and Royal Canadian identity tags were found. The two pilots and three resistance workers were arrested. It is understood they were forced to disclose the hiding place of the three airmen at Tilburg.

At 11.30 on Sunday Morning the 9th. July 1944 the three airmen had ventured downstairs and were having some breakfast when a knock came on the door. A party of seven Gestapo had arrived dressed in civilian clothes carrying arms. The leader went to No. 47, two entered No. 51 and four went to No. 49. The three Pilots with arms raised above their heads in surrender, were driven out of the house into the back yard, where they were made to stand against the wall and were immediately shot.

The Germans asked "Aunt Coba" for a cloth to cover the bodies. Without any thought for her own safety, she brought the Dutch Flag and draped the three bodies. She was arrested and sent to a concentration camp at Ravensbrook where she died in the gas chamber in February 1945.

The bodies of three airmen were taken to a crematorium at Vaght and, presumably to cover up the crime were cremated. However, unknown to the Germans, a Doctor Borman took photographs of the bodies, which were produced in evidence against the Germans when they were tried at Essen on the 11th to 26th June 1946 for the crime, when four Germans were sentenced to death.

The three resistance men caught at Tilburg were taken to the concentration camp at Vaght and shot. Curiously, the two Canadians caught at the same time, were taken prisoners of war and eventually reached their homeland. The wife of farmer Mr. J. Verhoven, where Ronald Walker was first found, was later shot by the Germans.

It is understood that the brother of "Aunt Coba" and his wife and family live in the house at 49, Diepenstraat, Tilburg, and on the wall where the airmen were shot is a memorial plaque to:

"Aunt Coba", Jacoba Pulskens.

Flight Leuit. Ronald Walker. Royal Air Force.

Flying Officer. Jack Nott. Royal Australian Air Force.

Flying Officer. Roy Carter. Royal Canadian Air Force.

I am told there is a Dutch book on the life of "Aunt Coba", which includes this passage:

"Three heroes fell there.

They made the sacrifice of their lives to God,

Liberty and our Fatherland.

We must treasure their memory.

Their names remain forever glorious.

Roy Carter,

Jaques Stewart Nott,

Ronald Walker."

"Aunt Coba" was the name given to a remarkable lady of some 60 years of age. She helped many aircrew to escape and also many Jews, illegal workers and other people fleeing from the Germans. Unfortunately she paid a big price with her life for the freedom of people.

All these facts came to light when Ron Low, Reunion Secretary for

83 Squadron, was researching into the losses of the Squadron. Subsequently the reunion took place at RAF Coningsby on Saturday 7th May 1983, which Vera and I were privileged to attend.

Also attending the Reunion were a Dutch party from Tilburg and relatives of the three Airmen from the U.K., Australia and Canada.

On Sunday morning the 8th. May 1983, a service was held in Coningsby Church which Vera and I attended. The flag that "Aunt Coba" had used for covering the three bodies, was actually dedicated and presented to the Church, and now hangs in the Airmen's Chapel.

Ron Low informs me that there is now a memorial plaque in the same Church at Coningsby, that is dedicated to the people involved in this story, but I have no further details.

"The Tragedy of War" has been included in the book of "MEMORIES", not only as a tribute to the people involved, but to all the countless people who gave their lives for the cause of freedom. Let us hope it was not given in vain!

Stanley Naylor.

"THE DAMBUSTERS".

Two years ago on the 16th May 1988, some of us were privileged to attend 617 Squadron Association's Re-Union to mark the 45th Anniversary of the breaching of the Ruhr Dams

In April this year I was in Germany and paid a visit to the Mohne Dam and here is a bit of history and some statistics on that famous Dam.

The Ruhr Dam Association was founded in 1899, its task: to decrease the damage caused by floods through the construction of Dams; to store up as much water as possible from the drainage of the Sauerland's higher regions during the winter months to fully utilize the electricity potential, and finally to feed water into the Ruhr River and its waterworks during the dry summer months.

The preliminary work began in 1905 and the foundations were completed in 1908. By the Autumn of 1910 the Dam had started to take shape and the damming up of the Mohne reservoir began in December 1912. Over 700 people who lived in 200 dwellings had to be resettled. The Official Inauguration took place on the 13th. July 1913, and the average yearly water flow through the Dam is 240 million cubic metres.

At their conference in Casablanca, President Roosevelt and Winston Churchill decided to destroy the German armament potential in the Ruhr Valley. During the first few months of 1943, heavy night attacks by the RAF caused severe damage to industrial cities on the Ruhr and the Rhine.

Air Marshall Sir Arthur Harris received instructions for a long prepared special task:- to effectively interrupt the water supply to the Ruhr industry in the summer of 1943, by destroying the Mohne, Eder and Sorpe Dams. A special unit of experienced flying crews was formed by Wing Commander Guy Gibson. It was called 617 Squadron, and consisted of 18 four engined Lancaster Bombers of the newest design and trains with over 2,000 bombs of special construction.

Mosquito Reconnaissance aircraft had, without being noticed, surveyed the water capacity of the reservoir and its weak defences. Then shortly before midnight on Sunday 16th May 1943, 617 Squadron started their attack on the Mohne Dam from the lake end, the first bomb dropped short and the second one dropped on the power station behind the wall of the Dam. The wall resisted the third and forth bombs, then Flight Lieutenant Maltby succeeded in releasing his special bomb (3.40 metre in diameter) exactly in front of the wall in between the towers, so that it exploded about 15 metres under the water surface.

The Mohne reservoir was filled with 133 million cubic metres of water at the time of the attack. The detonation of the special bomb and the increase of the water pressure broke the Dam to a depth of 20 meters and a breadth of 75 metres. Through the breach in the wall a flood wave 12 metres high ran with terrible effects into the lower Mohne valley, taking with it the ruins of the power station and houses and trees. A lot of damage was done to other power stations, saw mills, railway lines and factories.

The most regrettable - at least from the German point of view - was the destruction of a monastery - the house of the "Cistercian Order", which was confirmed by the pope in 1247 and reached great significance through the centuries.

The significance of the Mohne Dam was shown in the days after the catastrophe; five days after the attack, on the 22nd May, the reconstruction of the Dam commenced. Over 2,000 workers, amongst them numerous specialists, were put to work, so that in almost four months on the 2nd October 1943 the Dam, including the upper covering of reinforced concrete was ready. The adjoining plants, such as the power stations, the regulating basin and the bridges were left untouched, but the damming up of water in the reservoir could commence.

In November 1953 the regulating basin and the power stations were reinstalled, and in April 1955 the visitors were able to see water flowing over the Dam again. The water descends from a height of almost 40 metres through 105 vents each 2.50 metres wide as before the destruction, and presents the viewer with a picture of the strength of nature in a splendid setting. Not a scar or even a scratch in the huge Dam reminds one of the bad night of the year in 1943. Even though the reservoir has become an oasis of peace once again, one cannot forget the 56 aircrew who failed to return to RAF Scampton in the eight Lancasters that were lost. "WE WILL REMEMBER THEM".

Stanley Naylor.

GERMANY

On the same tour as visiting the Mohne Dam I also paid a visit to Berlin. By this time of course the Berlin wall had almost disappeared and was being sold at very high prices, never the less, I had to bring a few pieces back with me. In spite of one third of the city being destroyed during the war ,the 1948 blockade and, since 1961, the Berlin Wall dividing the city in two, the former Reich metropolis is vigorously alive, and well worth a visit should you be in that area.

It is not easy to visualise the enormity of the Barrier System on the Territory of the German Democratic Republic, even though one may have seen bits of it on various television programmes, so here are some statistics for you to ponder!

In 1980 these barrier systems included:-

1241 kilometres of mesh fencing

1241 kilometres of 6 metre wide ploughed and harrowed strip

1241 kilometres of vehicle track

1393 kilometres of border communications system

1002 kilometres of Hinterland security fence

793 kilometres of vehicle hazards - ditch/dragons teeth

366 kilometres of anti personnel minefields - approx 3,000 mines per km

364 kilometres of automatic firing devices SM70 = 34,800 explosive charges

297 approx prefabricated pill boxes

265 concrete observation towers

144 kilometres of double barbed wire fencing

212 kilometres of arclamps in front of villages

134 earth bunkers

92 kilometres of approx. dog runs, approx. 250 with approx. 1,000 dogs

59 command posts attached to observation towers

11 kilometres of wall in front of Niedersachsen village

The border disrupts: 27 Highways, 140 Secondary roads and numerous local - community roads and 32 railway lines. Before the opening up of the border it was only passable at 9 Highway crossings, 2 waterway crossings - river Eibe and Mittellandkanal, and 8 railway crossings.

Stanley Naylor.

RAF BINBROOK
by Joan Layng, Australia

The publicity surrounding Brian Edward's lone flight from Binbrook in Lincolnshire, England, back to Australia, in honour of his father who was one of the many thousands of aircrews to lose his life in the war-time bombing raids over Germany, brought back many memories for me of those far-off days. RAF Binbrook was the last of the twenty seven aerodromes that I inhabited during my four and a half years war service as a WAAF before being demobbed in 1946.

I was trained as a plotter in Fighter Command but I was posted to a Flying Training Unit near Newcastle-on-Tyne and didn't see much action apart from a few unidentified aircraft nosing round the shipping in the Tyne. So I re-mustered to what was called a Clerk/Special Duties (Watchkeeper) in Bomber Command. This was just about the time the heavy raids were being stepped up by Air Chief Marshall Harris, so I was to see plenty of action from then on!

Watchkeepers worked on shifts round the clock in the Operations Room which was buried deep underground. We manned a fairly complicate switchboard with internal lines to all parts of the Station and outside lines to Ack-Ack sites, Civil Defence and most important of all, Group Headquarters.

The hundreds of bomber aerodromes on the East coast were divided up into Groups, usually each peacetime permanent 'drome having two satellite 'dromes under its jurisdiction. We preferred being stationed on the satellites which consisted of rough and ready corrugated iron Nissen huts dotted over a wide area, so scattered, in fact, that we were all issued with bicycles to get from place to place. The discipline was less strict on those makeshift war-times 'dromes.

Each morning there would be a Group broadcast on the "scrambler" phone to ensure secrecy. When we were all hooked up we would get all the information on that night's raid, target Berlin, Essen, Mannheim or wherever, the route (I was terrified of making a mistake and sending 460 squadron aircraft from Binbrook on a leg away from the main stream, though this was highly unlikely as there was always a double check), the bomb load or if it was a "gardening" (mine laying) job the "vegetables" (mines) required. The estimated time of departure, time over target and time of arrival back were given and details of pathfinder over target.

Our job was to relay all this information to the various parties concerned - first the Station Commander, then the Flight Commander, out at Dispersal, the Signals Officer, Armoury, Navigation Officer, Intelligence, Photography, Meteorology sections, Messes etc. Then the great job of organising the total operation began. We also had to get what was called "Flimsies" out. These were lists of Recognition beacons all over the U.K., used as an aid for navigation for the returning bombers. The co-ordinates were changed every day. They were set out on rice paper so if the crew were shot down they could be eaten rather than fall into enemy hands!

Along one complete wall at the front of the Ops room was a big blackboard which looked rather like those used in the Stock Exchange. They had all the injformation of air-craft - J Johnny, S Sugar, X Xray etc and pilots names; ETD and ETA (Estimated Time of Departure and Estimated Time of Arrival) over target and ETA back at base. As take-off time approached we could hear the giant Merlin engines throbbing out at Dispersal, the planes ready to line up for their turn to taxi out and take off. The skies over the East coast filled with the steady drone of hundreds of Lancasters taking off from 'dromes such as Bimbrook, Wickenby and Scampton (of Dambusters fame) for some distant target far into enemy territory entailling hours of cold and nerve-wracking flight. During the raids to Berlin and other long flights we sat in Ops room far into the night anxiously awaiting news from the Control Tower of each safe arrival and the time would then be entered against that aircraft on the board. One never got used to the lonely blank spaces and you just hoped that the crew had either ditched in the sea and been picked up by Air Sea Rescue or perhaps bailed out safely.

It was not only over enemy territory that airmen came face to face with danger. There was the ever-present fear of mid-air collisions. Or sometimes freak accidents occured. I once witnessed a Stirling bomber and a fighter collide head on in mid-air. The Stirling just managed to avoid the Airmens Mess which was packed for the midday meal. The rear gunner's turret had sheared off on impact and was found some distance away from the rest of the wreckage. There were no survivors.

Sometimes our returning bombers were plagued by "intruders". These were German air-craft that came in with the main stream of returning bombers, so that Radar could not pick them up, and they proceeded to very accurately strike the 'drome.

On one such occasion I was due to go on night duty at 11.00pm. My friend and I had cycled seven miles to a wonderful apple Orchard in a little Suffolk village and returned with our bags full of apples ready to go on duty. When we arrived at the Ops room which, on the 'drome was in the same building as the Met office out near the Control Tower, we found that one of these intruders had dropped a bomb on the side of the building and demolished a corner of the Met office. Fortunately the WAAF on duty had been outside taking the hourly air temperatures and was not hurt. Our Ops room was a shambles and we were not able to go on duty that night. From then on we housed in temporary accomadation in a caravan out near the Dispersal huts. Fortunately we didn't have another intruder while I was stationed there!

But life was not all gloom and doom. There were Station dances and a bus left for Lincoln every night. There were some good films being shown in those days. I remember once being so enthralled by Ingrid Bergmann that we refused to leave before the end of the film and the bus went without us. We had to hitchhike back to camp!

Binbrook, of course, was an all Australian Station and I had never been amongst so many Australians before. We Watch-keepers held the rank of sergeant so we ate in the Sargeants Mess. There were only seven of us female sergeants and I remember being a trifle daunted at breakfast time having to face about six hundred somewhat scruffily dressed and very often unshaven males, while I toyed with a plate of putty goo that passed for porridge and a slice of greasy bacon floating in watery baked beans!

But I found the Aussies refreshingly informal and I sympathised with them when the bitter winds blew across the flat Lincolnshire countryside as they padded through the snow to their huts. One of them spoke longingly of his home in Queensland. Little did I know that eighteen years later I would settle with my family in the South West!

As I watched the News on television the other night and saw once again that lonely runway disappearing into the distance, my thoughts turned to the Binbrook I knew and the gallant men who, night after night, against almost overwhelming odds, braved those hostile, angry skies.

JOAN LAYNG. Ex. WAAF

No. 4 RAF HOSPITAL RAUCEBY

In 1939 as war clouds gathered it was realised that the small, well equipped hospital at RAF Cranwell would be inadequate to cope with the reception and treatment of patients on a large scale. On April 11th 1940, the Cranwell staff and patients took over the new (then) admissions unit which we know as Orchard House. Extensive alterations were made which included the equipping of two operating theatres.

In June the same year an urgent request was made for further accommodation. Consultations between the Hospital Committee, the board of Control, Ministry of Health and the Air Ministry led to the evacuation of the main hospital building and the Nurses' Home.

No. 4 General Hospital RAF Rauceby, had been planned as one of the principal RAF Hospitals and with hindsight we realise that its position was of vital importance to provide medical services for the multitude of RAF Stations that eventually covered Lincolnshire and beyond.

The very nature of the air warfare meant that many of the crew members were not only physically injured but also badly burnt. Rauceby so often became the first step on the long and painful road to recovery.

We must acknowledge the pioneering work of the resident surgeon, Sqd. Ldr. Fenton Braithwaite and his burns team and the surgeons and staff of the adjacent Orthopaedic Unit.

Sir Archibald McIndoe, whom everyone associates with East Grinstead and the Guinea Pig Club, also visited and operated at RAF Rauceby. A number of cases were transferred to East Grinstead from Rauceby for further surgery.

At the height of the war there were some one thousand beds in use and another one thousand in store to be used in the event of invasion or extensive bombing.

That the hospital was busy can be seen by the statistics - for example, in 1943, nearly 4,400 operations were performed and over 23,000 cases treated. Men and women of all nationalities passed through these portals and it became a familiar sight to see patients in the locality in their ill-fitting uniform.

A number of young men, who became legends in their own lifetimes, had occassion to be patients of Rauceby. For instance:-

Wing Commander Guy Gibson VC., who was here shortly before he went on his last fatal mission; Flight Sergeant John Hannah who won his VC., at the age of eighteen in 1940, (sadly, he was discharged from the RAF in 1942 and died in 1947); Air Chief Marshal Sir Augustus Walker, who, as Commanding Officer at Syerston, lost an arm in an airfield accident.

Happy (albeit painful) memories abound from the most exalted rank to the lowliest 'erk'. Morale was high and spirits lightened by the provision of entertainments in the form of shows and dances which were held weekly. Many famous names trod the boards of Rauceby stage and the weekly dances with music provided by the hospital's own dance band 'The Medicos', were popular with both those at the hospital and local residents.

Rauceby fortunately escaped damage at the hands of the enemy but accidently suffered severe damage to its ballroom. On Whit Monday night in 1945 a fire was discovered at 3.00am. This must have been burning for several hours as the wood panelling and highly polished floors were well alight. Despite the efforts of hospital and local fire brigades the room was completely gutted. It did not rise from the flames until 1948.

The feeling of close companionship shared by the medical staff led to the formation of a unique club simply known as "The RAUCEBY CLUB". It was formed by Wg Cdr Eric Jewsbury and included all Medical Staff who had worked or had connections with RAF Hospital Rauceby. Its membership list reads as a "Who's Who" of the medical profession as many of these doctors and surgeons went on to achieve eminence in their particular fields. The Club was unique in that it was the only one of its kind ever formed. Its annual dinners, which continued well into the 1980's, became legendary.

RAF Hospital Rauceby was in existence for a comparitevly short period (1940 to 1947) and whilst much of the work carried out had been routine, a fair amount had been, by the nature of the injuries sustained, both experimental and life-saving. Many of the techniques developed then are still in use today.

This RAF Hospital has been a focal point during a unique period of Lincolnshire history and many more people had cause to be grateful for its existence. All that is left are memories and records in writing with photographs that bear silent witness to the bravery and fortitude of the patients and the humanity and skills of the staff.

LET US NOT FORGET!

by Mrs Gwyneth Stratten.

THE LETTER
by A.H. White, Boston

I was looking through the rack for letters; letters from home, anywhere. The April sun made the Nissen hut just a wee bit hot, or so I thought; but somehow I knew I was kidding myself; the sweat damping my forehead and making my hands sticky was not the heat. I felt clammy, sticky, suffocated and my feet hurt a little from standing too long on a metal ladder; my hands were sore and grazed from handling a hot engine. "Blast the bloody letters", I murmured; but the rack held me as tightly as though I were a fly and the rack a paper - seemed crazy, sticky fly, plain paper, should be the other way round I thought. Queer that; I chuckled; it hurt did that chuckle and The Letter must be there - it must be in the pigeon hole marked "T" - it was there; "Christ Almighty". The postmark, the writing, was here. Jack had said, last night, the letter would come...

Dimly through a pearly clammy mist, I saw myself walking across the sand from "Roger" to "Sugar". Roger had "run up". I had watched her engines carefully during it, heard Keith say "bang on", and left the crew to sort themselves out. "Doc", the mid-upper, would share out the chocolate, begin once again the interminable polishing of his turret perspex, Bill, the engineer, have a last look - over oxygen bottles, his log sheets, and make sure to borrow a pencil - everybody lent pencils to Bill - while Keith, the skipper, acted as referee in a rough and tumble between rear guns and bomb-aimer.

The navigator wouldn't be along yet anyway - he usually arrived barely in time to take-off; arrived hot and red about the gills with a great canvas bag stuffed to the brim with maps, charts, rules, computers, as though he was preparing to lecture a class of ruffians in some obtuse mathematical formulae, full of fuss and bother.

As I walked the light softened as a cloud obscured the last rays of a dying sun, the tossing conifers to the rear of the dispersal swished lazily in a gusty breeze, their delicate upper fingers losing themselves in a blue velvet of dusk in the east, while a startled rabbit made a brown evanescent blur as it scudded over the sandy soil. "Sugar" seemed to merge with the trees, like a gaunt black monster airing leathery cold wings after a storm; creeping to the darkness on spidery legs ending in huge black circular paws.

Jack was standing by the concrete's rim, having a last smoke and a quiet chat with his crew. There was something very quiet, and still, about Jack. We always ate together on his non-flying days, and talked of the Yorkshire from which each of us had come; of home, Yorkshire "cards", Haworth, Bingley, Ilkley Moor, Leeds, and his eyes would relax into soft quiet pools as happy memories stilled that which was happening now.

"Everything O.K. Jack", I said, "Not bad", he replied. "What's she like Chalky?" "well", I replied, "I only really know the engines, and they're bang on - Roger's my baby - but so far as I know she's no vices, left wing low two trips ago; but you might stop your "boy" from playing in that turret, he'll bugger it up". We strolled round to the rear. "Sandy" Powell seemed to be having quite a time - ammo strewn all around the concrete and Sandy cocking and unloading his guns as though he was a lad playing with a meccano. He was a lad, barely twenty; his helmet was perched on his head like a parrot on a rolling beer bottle, his tongue was just peeping out, and he had the guilty look of a boy caught stealing apples."

"Leave 'em alone", I begged, "some **real** armourers have worked on 'em today". Jack laughed, and Sandy swore. "Better leave 'em alone", Jack said. "I've got post-war plans".

"Post war plans". Somehow I felt chilled and angry; the bantering humour rolling like a lead ball into my stomach, leaving my head old, weary and miserable. "Post war plans" - he'd actually mentioned a future, he, who only that morning had told me of another Jack Towers waiting to be born. "She hates telegrams", he said, "So she'll send a letter".

I saw 'Roger' off. Keith held her down nicely for the full length of the runway, gained plenty of speed and let her fly off. Jack seemed to lift 'Sugar' off - not his usual performance at all - and climb in steps.

By now it was dark. I wished he hadn't mentioned post war plan. The kites circled, gaining height, there was a throb in the air, in the ground, in one's chest, faintly disturbing; a feeling as of unreality as though one were under anaesthesia, unable to remember a past or to imagine a future.

Present, yes, that was it, present; no post war plans; just "presents" maybe a lot, maybe a few; noise, wind, sand, take offs, and sleep. It wasn't my turn for night flying anyway.

I awoke, after a time, and looked around the nissan, Ginger's bed was empty, so I lay idly counting the returns as the pressing throb of sound grew with each landing; it all lapsed into a dream shattered by Ginger's climb into his creaking bed. "All back Ging"? I questioned, "Sugar's in a field the other side of the woods - rear gunner's got the chop". There was a growling "get to sleep", from the others. All I could see was a helmet perched like a parrot on a rolling beer bottle - just like Sandy. "I'll bet he was undressing on the approach", said Ginger reading my thoughts; "If he hadn't have come forward he'd have walked away - she broke in two by the rear door".

Jack was in the mess next day. He didn't talk about Yorkshire. "Jack's leaving mid-upper and going rear - when he's sober - but I reckon we'll get some leave in first". "See you when we get back - same time, same place".

Jack seemed tired after his leave; his eyes as dead as a street walker's. He was still waiting for a letter. Funny, but we always seemed to meet at the letter rack, and we always seemed to be first in the queue.

I kept my eyes open for his name on the Battle Orders, Keith and "Roger" never seemed to miss - maybe they were giving Jack a rest - but no, he soon came down to "W - Willy".

It was my turn to see them back that night, so I made a bed by the phone and waited, while the erks scrounged fuel for the stove. The night was calm and black - ideal for a mine-laying stooge - so I settled down to a placid snooze. At least there wouldn't be any trouble tonight; all my blokes well seasoned and able to cope with anything; no worries; if only that damned "Post War Plans" would fade!

The phone shattered the stillness, rest, and warmth as effectively as a rocket through a window; the door was slammed ajar, leaning crazily on its hinges, and we listened in the black night for the throbbing crescendo. But there was little time, for soon the first fire splitting shadow rolled towards us with a whistle of brakes and jangle of undercarriage, its red and green wing-tip lights swaying fascinatingly nearer to that red light at which started our job - signalling each to its appropriate bed, there to refuel throughout the night and clear whatever un-serviceability we could for the morrow.

Soon most of us were sweating, swearing, cursing sand, the Germans, the war, everything in the universe - a universe bounded by black shapes blurred on a black velvet night, gales of wind from propellers speeding for manouvering and the ever present sand gritting between teeth, irritating ears and eyes.

But there was no "Willy" to refuel. I waited an hour. "Post War Plans" - quiet eyes - Yorkshire. It seemed futile to ask, yet I did. "You'll not be getting Willy sarge" the voice on the phone answered. "Right Sir", I replied, and rang off. The sweat dried. The runway lights were quenched, and everything became cold and dark; the world shrank into things which were stumbled over and gave only pain; it was narrow, confined, with a memory way back a long dark tunnel.

Dawn came, Breakfast, morning inspections, sorting out the best of "Willey's" ground equipment.

I took hold of the letter, wondered.......... shall I write? But I couldn't hold it. I put it back in the rack. I couldn't write to her - worse than having a baby of your own.

The letter was there next day, and the next, and then I saw the "discip" bloke. "For God's sake do your job and collect Tower's mail" I snapped He looked shocked and angry. As I walked away I fancy he tapped forehead significantly.

A.H. White.

WHERE IGNORANCE IS BLISS
by Denys Brown
(ex Air Signaller - 1942-6)

Sgt. "Sam" Small RCAF, and crew, joined 12 Sqdn. early in July 1944. On the 11th, they carried out their first duty at Wickenby, a Night Cross Country including bombing and airfiring for 6 hours 10 minutes. The main object of this was probably to ensure that we could safely find our way home in the dark.

The next night, Sam and I were ordered to accompany the Flight Commander, S/L Brown, on the real thing, an operation to the railway yard, at Tours in France. We were in distinguished company. As I recall it, the Gunnery, Navigation and Bombing Leaders were all there.

You may well ask what was I doing there? At that time I had already over 500 hours air signalling time and in any case it was right for Sam to have his own operator for us both to learn what the real duties could be like. At any rate I was excited at the prospect and so very conscientious at my daily inspection that day.

I don't remember much of the outward trip. The W/O's duties were in any case a bit "in the dark" and attached to the radio (R1154/1155), so that he wouldn't see much, going in. In any case, flying with "Sir", I wasn't going to get caught out doing anything wrong.

Arrived at the Target I was fascinated .

As the flares went down, the whole railway complex was lit up almost like daylight and one could clearly see the figures on the ground, haring for cover. Standing in the astrodome, I forgot all about my search area, being far too interested in the general proceedings below. If there was any flak, I didn't notice it.

Then we started on the bombing run. It was obvious that the bombing leader intended to impress the boss. "Bomb doors open!" There goes another flare. "Left, left." Will you look at that waggon getting airborne. "Steady, steady." "Bomb the green markers".

This last from the Master Bomber who wasn't the least concerned at interrupting 12 sqdn's Bombing Leader. So "Round again Skip." and off to starboard we go, to turn back in to the stream and "Throw Six and Start Again".

The Master Bomber had lots to say that night and seemed to think of it just as we were lined up on the target. So two or three times this "Round Again" routine was repeated before the final "Bombs Away, Bomb Doors Closed".

How interesting it was! What a lot to tell the bods when I get back. Six and a half hours after take off, we landed and I walked away in a heroic glow to my bed.

It wasn't until several ops later that I realised what a "dice" we had had, wandering around the sky on our own and re-entering the bomber stream like that. Fighters? Flak?

Where ignorance is bliss, etc.

© Denys Brown 1992

This story was given to us many years ago by the late Air Chief Marshal, Sir Augustas Walker, GCB., CBE., DSO., DFC., AFC.

Gus, as he was so affectionately known to us all, wrote this story in 1960 and, I believe, used it in one of his speeches. But it is relevant at the time of writing, as I have just read a book on operation "Sea Lion", that gives the German version, but it was not written until 1980, details later.

BATTLE OF BRITAIN 1960

1 Twenty years ago the climax of the Battle of Britain was being fought in the sky over Britain, and with it the fate of this country and, no doubt, that of the free world was being decided.
2 That Victory was won and with it the tide turned so that, although many more battles were to be fought throughout the world, the ultimate defeat of the enemy was ensured.
3 Acting on Hitler's order, the German General Staff drew up the orders for operation "Sea-Lion", the plan for the invasion of this country, to be launched in the middle of September 1940. The essential prerequisite for the operation to be undertaken was the achievement of air superiority by the Luftwaffe over the English Channel. Historians have revealed how Goering's Air Force failed to meet the demands of Hitler's admirals and generals.
4 In those few weeks of endeavour, those few hundred fighter pilots had earned for the Royal Air Force an immortality that will stand with Trafalgar and Waterloo.
5 Each year, and especially this 20th Anniversary, we seek to celebrate with the public that great victory, and it is a measure of the public's knowledge of the historic place the Battle has in our heritage that they continue to support the ceremonies planned in Battle of Britain Week.
6 The Royal Air Force is indeed fortunate that it has always the unstinted and enthusiastic help of the Royal Air Forces Association in keeping alive the memories of those vital weeks. As each generation grows up it becomes more and more important to pass

on to them the glorious part of our Service so that all those who have the honour to serve in the Royal Air Force can hold themselves with pride.

Gus Walker. 7th September 1960.

Details of the book I mentioned:
    INVASION written by Kenneth Macksey
    Published by: Arms and Armour Press Ltd., 1980
    A Corgi Book ISBN 0 552 11830 3.

Stanley Naylor.

HORNCASTLE - LOUTH BUS SERVICE
THROUGH THE WOLDS

The Lincolnshire Wolds are a source of beauty spots and real natural countryside, that rise a mere 500 feet (153 metres) above sea level. The Wolds proves that Lincolnshire is not completely flat, but has wooded valleys and rolling hills. Some of the valleys hide farmsteads complete with houses and small church. Most villages have a Church , and also a Pub where the traveller would find some kind of refreshment, even if it was only in liquid form.

This bus route would be an ideal Sunday Afternoon excursion by car, preferably in the summer, or a nice sunny day in the Spring or Autumn. Definitely not recommended in the Winter, as I can recall having some treacherous journeys in this area travelling on ice and snow. There were weeks when some of the roads were closed, blocked with snow drifts.

The Springtime was really exhilarating to see the new born lambs frisking in the fields, the hedgerows springing to life, leaves forming on the trees, flowers, especially snowdrops, blooming in the well kept gardens and the corn now showing a deep green.

The Autumn sees things changing. Huge machines are harvesting the now golden corn, the hedges are trimmed, the flowers are wilting, the lambs are almost fully grown, but the leaves on the trees are varying shades of colour and will soon be falling to the ground.

How do I know all this? Not only am I a country lad, but I have traversed this route many times as the driver of the bus, mostly on Wednesdays, and on a few occasions on a Saturday. One journey, Horncastle to Louth and return on Wednesdays, and twice on Saturdays. The years of my involvement was from 1978 to 1983.

The job entailed taking children to school for 9.00am then heading for Horncastle, to depart precisely at 9.30am from outside Boots in the Market Place.

Horncastle is one of the principal towns in this agricultural area, market days being Thursday and Saturday, where we find various stalls selling their wares. The town stands on the banks of both the rivers Bain and Waring. Banovallum is understood to be a Roman site on which the town was built and that name is now carried by a local school. Horncastle is a busy town with a good shopping centre and some fine Inns where the weary traveller can find refreshment and rest.

Our journey commences at the Market Place and turns left down the one-way street, sometimes this was not possible due to parked vehicles, so we have to go down to Lincoln road and turn left. This takes us down to the traffic lights, turn left on the A153 heading for Louth.

I'm not sure of the year, but around the end of the 1950's beginning of the 1960's the river Bain overflowed and flooded the town. So as we approach the traffic lights on the Lincoln road and look across the river, we see on a house wall, a high water mark that will give some indication of the depth of water pouring through the town on that particular day. If we turn left down the one-way street from the Market Place, the river will now be on our right and we will be able to stop and see the mark on our left.

Leaving Horncastle on the A153 our first village is West Ashby, where we see a lovely old church which could well be worth a visit. We don't have time to stop, of course, because we have to keep to a timetable.

Travelling along the A153, we note there are long stretches of straight road, with wide grass verges. We don't stay on this road very long after leaving West Ashby, but turn right at the crossroads. Immediately in front is another straight road, which is not much wider than the bus, the bus being just over eight feet wide. The road goes down a steep hill over a narrow bridge crossing the river Waring, then climbs out of the valley bearing left for Fulletby. Now a car will not be troubled so much with the ups and downs of these valleys, as the Bedford buses that were used on this route. Neither would the modern Bus/Coach have any problems today, they have the power and the brakes to negotiate any steep hills with ease.

The focal point in Fulletby is St. Andrew's Church, and on leaving the village there is a high radio mast, but I have never established its purpose. As the 'T' junction is approached, on a clear day, in the distance can be seen the villages of Salmondby and Tetford. If we are really lucky we might see Somersby and Bag Enderby at 1.00 o'clock, using the clock face for direction.

Turning left at the junction, there is an excellent view on the left before descending one of the steepest hills on the route: Staining Hill is 16% (1 in 6) which drops into Belchford. As we round a left-hand bend on leaving this Wolds village and get on the straight piece of road, it is often possible to see Lincoln Cathedral in the far distance at about 12.00 o'clock.

On the left immediately over the crossroads at Foxendales are the South Wold Hunt kennels, often the hounds would be seen exercising on the broad grass verges ahead. The road is still only wide enough for the bus, so the grass verge had to be used when meeting other traffic.

Our next 'port of call' is the Village Hall at Hemingby, where, the bus is scheduled to arrive at 9.55am. Not an easy time to keep, even in the summer, and impossible in the winter, but passengers would still be waiting, come rain or shine! Hardy folk inhabit the Wolds, nothing deters them from their weekly trip to market.

Hemingby is on the bank of the river Bain, part of St. Margaret's Church dates back to 1764 and, I believe, was extensively re-built in 1895. There are five Almshouses that were built in 1727 as a school and hospital.

Leaving Hemingby on an almost straight road that rises to 400 feet above sea level, we pass Hemingby High House on the left and Asterby Grange on the right. At the 'T' junction we turn left for Goulceby where is an almost modern church, rebuilt in 1908 and Three Horse Shoe Inn that looks rather quaint and most definitely ancient. I would say that Spring is the best time to visit Goulceby to have a meander around the village to see snowdrops, violets and bluebells blooming, plus a local Nature Reserve with coloured rocks and chalk.

Passing through Asterby we arrive at the main Horncastle/Louth road where we turn left, travelling a short distance then turn right into Scamblesby. The school is our stop, due at 10.10am but I know we are running late. Another Church and also a Methodist Chapel are passed as we head back to the main road, A153. We are now faced with Cawkwell hill, although only 1 in 10, it is very difficult to climb as it is not possible to get a good run before starting to climb. We chug slowly to the top, arriving safely with a sigh of relief, the height now above sea level is 139m (457 feet).

At the top of Cawkwell Hill we cross Bluestone Heath Road. (I'll refer back to this road later). Continuing our journey, we will see the entrance to Cadwell Park Race Circuit on the right. The circuit was opened in 1936 and some weekends it is possible to catch a glimpse of cars or motorcycles on the track.

Round a right hand bend and at the fork the main road goes left, but we go straight ahead down the hill into Tathwell. The pond, small stream and topiary, along with St. Vedast's Church make Tathwell a picturesque village in the heart of the Wolds.

We proceed out of Tathwell and turn left at the crossroads, joining the A153 once more again at Raithby. As we proceed down into Louth, over on the left is Hubbards Hills. This is rather a strange name for this area, because it is more of a valley through which flows the river Lud. The area is well worth a visit and is ideal for picnic.

At the traffic lights in Louth we turn left into Upgate, then a short distance turn right to the Market Place, where usually all the passengers depart from the bus, which carries on to the Bus Station to park for nearly three hours. During this time I would walk round the stalls, have 'forty winks', a sarnie, cup of tea and a chat to other bus drivers. At around 1.15pm, some of the passengers would be wending their way to the bus, heavy laden with shopping and very pleased to sit down and rest their weary feet.

But before we leave Louth on our return journey, there are a few items of interest about this town which are noteworthy.

Market days are Wednesday and Saturdays. Early closing is on Thursdays.

St. James's Church has the tallest spire of any parish church in England: 90m (295 feet). This is higher than Boston Stump by some 23 feet. 82.5m (272 feet) Louth Church is reputed to have been built from the profits of the wool and cloth industry, Boston Stump is reputed to have been built on wool, not literally, of course, but from the profits selling wool.

In Westgate, are Georgian houses, and also the Wheatsheaf Inn from an earlier period. In Westgate Place you will find the house where Alfred Tennyson, the well known Lincolnshire poet, lodged during the years he was a pupil at King Edward VI School. Bridge Street has a splendid Regency terrace, and Little Eastgate has the 1866 Market Hall, opposite is the 1854 Town Hall. The former 1835 Wesleyan Centenary Church has been transformed internally into the Louth Methodist Church. The Playhouse Cinema in Cannon Street was once the Congregational Church. The late eighteenth century Mansion House in Upgate is the Public Library, and the timber-framed 16th century Cromwell House is a restaurant.

So the Horncastle bus departs promptly at 1.30pm from the bus station, travelling down the one-way to the market place, where most of the passengers board the bus and they are returned, complete with an enormous amount of shopping, to their respective villages.

We arrive in Horncastle at the appointed time of 2.30pm. Now all that remains for me to do is return to the school where I deposited a load of children in the morning, transport them safely to their individual houses, return the bus to the depot, and so another day's work is completed.

I'm sure the bus route from Horncastle through the Villages mentioned finishing in Louth, will prove to be an interesting tour by car. Linger a short while in the villages and talk to the locals, discover more about the history of the Lincolnshire Wolds, they have a lot to offer a traveller.

Here are a couple of things to look out for, of which I don't have too much information.

Belchford: I often used to wonder why youthful boys and girls would be joining the bus, or disembarking in this village. Then I learned of the Ruckland Youth Hostel, some miles distance from Belchford. For further information try the Post Office.

The Viking Way: Not being keen on walking, the Viking Way holds no interest for me, but these details may be of interest to the reader.

The Viking Way was opened in 1977 and stretches from the Humber Bridge through the Wolds down to Leicestershire. The Way is marked by posts at intervals bearing a symbol of a Viking Horned Helmet. The bus route crosses the Way in the Villages of Asterby, Goulceby, Scamblesby, Belchford and Fulletby. The route therefore, brings hikers close to the Hostel at Ruckland.

Further information from East Lindsey District Council Offices at Horncastle and Louth.

Bluestone Heath Road: This road is a very interesting drive starting in the north at Rothwell, take the road to Binbrook. On arriving at Binbrook, watch the signs carefully, you want the Kelstern Road. Passing through Kelstern, go straight over the A631. Arriving at the A157, you should have Burgh-on-Bain on your right and Welton le Wold on your left. Turn left on the A157 and immediately turn right heading for Cadwell and the A153.

On arriving at the A153, you will have Cawkwell Hill on your right and Cadwell Race Track over the main road on your left. Cross straight over the A153 heading for South Orsby, which is not a straight route, but is direct, don't deviate anywhere. You will pass Scamblesby over on your right, Oxcombe and Ruckland on your left, Belchford and Tetford over on your right. Look out for lay-byes, they make good observation points. One on your right near Belchford has some useful information. Carry on through South Ormsby, huge Hall on your right, over the crossroads and down the A16 where the Bluestone Road ends.

I hope you have enjoyed your tour of the Wolds.

Stanley Naylor, July 1996.

KITCHEN PRAYER

****

Bless my little kitchen, Lord,
I love its every nook
and bless me as I do my work,
Wash pots and pans and cook.

May the meals that I prepare,
Be seasoned from above,
With thy blessing and thy grace,
But most of all thy love.

As we partake of earthly food,
The table thou hast spread,
We'll not forget to thank thee Lord,
For all our daily bread.

So bless my little kitchen, Lord,
And those who enter in;
May they find naught but joy and peace
and happiness therein.

AMEN

****

POTATOES

From over 50 varieties grown in this country, here are the top seven.

1) **DESIREE**: Red skinned with yellow flesh. An all round potato and very good when boiled, baked or chipped.

2) **MARIS PIPER**: The most widely grown maincrop variety and suitable for most cooking uses.

3) **CARA**: Large and round and particularly good for baking. They have a white skin with pink eyes.

4) **PENTLAND CROWN**: A popular variety whose flesh tends to be less floury than other main crop varieties.

5) **KING EDWARD**: Named after King Edward VII. This potato is one of the best known varieties. King Edward potatoes were being produced way back in the 1930s - and perhaps even before that - but they have always been a very good eating potato. The flesh is very floury which makes it ideal for mashing or roasting.

6) **PENTLAND SQUIRE**: A potato with a very white skin and flesh. Has particularly good cooking qualities, especially when baked.

7) **ROMANO**: Another red-skinned variety similar to Desiree, both in appearance and cooking suitability.

All seven are 'maincrop' varieties, available from September to April/May. You should be able to find one of the above best suited to your needs.

NEW POTATOES

New potatoes are very different from the maincrop varieties, they are in fact known as 'Earlies'. English grown new potatoes are available from May to July.

'First Earlies' are picked fresh and in the shops within 24 hours, these are varieties such as Home Guard, Arran Comet and Pentland Javelin.

There is an easy way to test for freshness. Take a new potato and rub the skin with your thumb, if it comes away easily and feels damp, then you can be sure that you have got a fresh potato. To get the full benefit from that freshness, only buy new potatoes in the amounts you are going to use immediately. You will find that new potatoes do not keep fresh much beyond two - or perhaps three days. They do damage easily and soon go discoloured, so beware when buying them.

All one needs to do to prepare new potatoes for cooking, is to put them in a bucket of water and scrub them with a stiff yard brush. If they are a day or two old, then they may need scraping with a knife.

The best way to cook new potatoes is to boil them whole. Simply put them into boiling water and cook for about 15 minutes. Salt can be added to the boiling water and a sprig of mint added also gives a unique flavour. Butter can be added to them once they are cooked.

Now main crop potatoes will keep through the winter, but they must be stored in a paper bag, not polythene. Always keep them in a cool and dry place.

Exposure to light turns potatoes green, frost can damage them too. Avoid storing near to strong smelling items such as petrol, paraffin, paint and detergents etc, because potatoes taint so easily.

Living in the heart of a Potato country, I could not resist including a few ways of preparing and cooking some special dishes.

ROAST POTATOES

Ingredients:

2lb (0.90kg) potatoes   3oz (56.70g) butter/margarine

Peel potatoes and dry thoroughly. Make the butter/margarine very hot in a baking tin. Place potatoes in the tin, baste well and bake in a hot oven, turn frequently for about 45 minutes until crisp and brown.

SAVOURY POTATOES

Ingredients:

1lb (0.45kg) potatoes	½lb (0.23kg) onions
1 pint (0.568 litres) milk	1 egg
Margarine	salt and pepper

Fill a greased pie-dish with alternative layers of sliced raw potatoes and onions. Season with salt and pepper. Cover with three parts of milk to one part of water and cook in a moderate oven for one hour. Can be served as a vegetable with cold meat.

TEMPERATURES

Heat of oven	Electricity		Gas Mark
	°C	°F	
slow	120	250	1
	150	300	2
very moderate	170	325	3
moderate	180	350	4
moderately hot	190	375	5
hot	200	400	6
	220	425	7
very hot	230	450	8
	260	500	9

POTATO BROWNIES

makes one dozen

Ingredients:

4oz (113.40g) plain chocolate (broken)

4oz (113.40g) soft brown sugar

2oz (56.70g) potatoes (cooked)

4oz (113.40g) butter/margarine

2oz (56.70g) chopped walnuts

4oz (113.40g) self-raising flour

2 tablespoons of milk

2 eggs

pinch of salt

Place the butter/margarine and chocolate in a bowl and stand over a saucepan of hot water until melted, stirring occasionally.

Remove bowl from the heat and mix in potatoes and sugar then leave to cool.

Mix flour and salt in a separate bowl, make a hole in the centre of the flour and pour in the chocolate mixture. Mix it all together.

Beat the eggs in a cup, and add to the mixture with the walnuts. Add enough milk to make a soft consistency.

Pour into a greased 11" x 7" (28cm x 18cm) cake tin and cook for thirty minutes at 375°F, 190°C or Gas Mark 5.

Leave to cool in the tin before cutting into 12 squares.

POTATO SCONES

Ingredients:

6oz (170.1g) cooked mashed potatoes

2oz (56.7g) butter/margarine

5oz (141.75g) flour

2 teaspoons baking powder

½ teaspoon salt

½ teaspoon milk

Steam potatoes and mash with a spoon. Mix together flour, baking powder and salt. Rub in fat and mix in potatoes. Add sufficient milk to make soft dough. Turn on to a floured board. Roll out in to round ½ inch thick. Bake in a hot oven 450°F, 230°C or Gas Mark 8 for about 15 minutes.

Cut in triangles and serve hot with butter/margarine.

POTATOES WITH CHEESE

Ingredients:

1lb (0.45kg) potatoes boiled

3oz (85.05g) grated cheese

1oz (23.35g) butter/margarine

2 tablespoons milk

Browned breadcrumbs (your choice how many!)

Pepper and salt to taste.

Mash potatoes while hot, add milk, seasoning, half the butter/margarine and cheese. Grease a pie dish, stir in the crumbs rather thickly and put in mixture. Put remaining fat and cheese on the top. Bake for half an hour and serve hot.

LINCOLNSHIRE HOT POT

Ingredients:

6 chops - meat of your choice

4 kidneys

8oz (225g) onions, peeled and sliced

8oz (225g) carrots, peeled and sliced

8oz (225g) turnips, peeled and sliced

Sticks of celery, cleaned and sliced

Salt, pepper and flour

1 pint (575/600ml) stock

½ pint (275/300ml) best beer

potatoes - quantity to your choice.

Trim the meat so as not to have too much fat. Put in the bottom of the pot some of the chops and kidneys. covered with some of the onions, carrots, turnips, celery and potatoes.

Fill up the pot with layers of these ingredients, putting a good layer of potatoes on the top.

Add the stock and beer, salt and pepper to taste, add water to nearly fill the pot, a little flour could be sprinkled on centre layers.

Cook in a hot oven for three hours. Watch for the pot boiling over, be careful not to fill too much, the stock and beer might be enough without water, depends on the size of the pot.

LINCOLNSHIRE DOUGHCAKE

Ingredients:

1lb (0.45kg) strong plain flour

5½oz (155.92g) brown sugar

1lb 2oz (510.30g) currants and sultanas

9oz (255.15g) water

1oz (28.35g) bakers yeast   5oz (141.75g) lard

Nutmeg and lemon essence   ¼oz (7.09g) salt

Activate yeast by placing in a 2lb (0.90kg) pudding basin with ½oz brown sugar, 1½oz water. Warm at blood heat. Mix these ingredients with a fork while the pudding basin is placed in a bowl containing water also at about blood heat. The mixture will rise and fall activating a lot of bubbles.

Wash fruit and soak in water for five minutes.

Place flour in a bowl, add salt, sugar, lard, nutmeg and lemon essence.

When yeast has activated, add rest of the 9oz of water so hot that you can just bear your fingers in it. Then add the yeast to the dry ingredients, dissolving the lard and sugar with your hand.

Mix into a dough and add the warm fruit. Prove in a warm place wrapped in a warm tea cloth for ¾ hour.

Then knock down (flour your hands) and leave for another ½ hour.

Make four dough cakes at about 15oz (425.25g). Place in greased 1lb (0.45kg) bread tins, when proved to double their size (while keeping them warm) bake at about 350°F, 180°C or Gas Mark 4 for 45 minutes.

Harold Wilkinson RAFA

OLD LINCOLNSHIRE GINGER CAKE

Bring to the boil these ingredients:

7oz (198.45g) golden syrup

3½oz (99.23g) margarine

⅛oz (3.55g) ground ginger

⅛oz (3.55g) mixed spice

Whisk together until light:

3½oz (99.23g) sugar

3½oz (99.23g) eggs (approx 2 whole eggs)

Add the two mixtures together.

Bring to the boil 4¼oz (120.49g) of milk.

Add the milk to the above mixtures, then add 7oz strong plain flour and ⅛oz of bicarbonate of soda. Mix and blend in smoothly avoiding any lumps.

Split into 3" x 5" papered tins and bake at approximately 325°F, 170°C or Gas Mark 3 for 40 minutes

Harold Wilkinson RAFA

Useful conversion guide for imperial and metric weights.

Grammes to ounces - divide grammes by 29 - gives approx ozs.

Example:

250g divide by 29 = 8½oz

125g divide by 29 = 4¼oz

Ozs/lbs to grammes:

½lb/8oz multiply by 29 = 232g

3oz multiply by 29 = 87g

mg   1000 milligrams = 1 gram
g   1000 grammes = 1 kilogramme
kg   100 kilograms = 1 quintal
        10 quintals = 1 tonne

Use grammes to buy sweets etc

Use kilograms to buy flour, potatoes etc.

Use tonnes to buy coal

BAKEWELL TART

Ingredients:

3oz (85.05g) sugar	3oz (85.05g) butter/margarine
¼ pint of milk (142ml)	½ teaspoon of almond essence
3oz (85.05g) cake crumbs	Grated rind from half a lemon
A squeeze of lemon juice	2 eggs

Strawberry jam (jam can be your choice)

Shortcrust pastry

Mix the fat and sugar to a cream, add the beaten eggs and grated lemon rind. Slowly add the milk required up to ¼ of a pint, then the cake crumbs. The almond essence and lemon juice can be added.

Stir all ingredients lightly to a soft consistency.

Line a pie-plate with pastry and cover with a layer of jam, spread the mixture evenly over the jam.

Bake in a hot oven - 425°F, 220°C or Gas Mark 7 - for about ten minutes, to set the pastry, then reduce the heat and cook for another 40 to 50 minutes, until the filling is set, risen firm and golden brown.

SLAB CAKE

Ingredients:

1lb (0.45kg) Self-raising flour	8oz (226.8g) margarine
4oz (113.4g) each of currants, sultanas and stoned raisins.	
4oz (113.4g) mixed peel	8oz (226.9g sugar
½ level teaspoon of cinnamon	
½ level teaspoon of mixed spice	Pinch of salt
14 tablespoons of milk	2 eggs

Mix flour, salt and spices together. Mix margarine and sugar together until fluffy and light, then beat in eggs, one at a time until thoroughly mixed in the margarine and sugar substance.

Now add fruit, peel and milk to all above ingredients, mixing well.

Line an 8 inch (20.32cm) square cake tin with greaseproof paper and brush all around inside with melted fat - margarine or butter - your choice.

Spread the mixture evenly in the tin.

Bake in a moderate oven, 300°F, 150°C or Gas Mark 2 between 1¾ and 2¼ hours

Remove from oven, turn out cake from the tin, strip off the paper and leave to cool.

It is, however, very tasty when still hot.

DAMPER (Australian Bush)

Ingredients:

3 cups of Self-raising flour, plus some extra.

1½ teaspoons of salt   3oz (85.05g) butter/margarine

½ cup of milk   ½ cup of water

Mix flour and salt in a bowl, rub in butter/marg until mixture resembles breadcrumbs, fairly even in size.

Make a well in the dry ingredients, add milk and water together, mix lightly with a knife in a cutting motion. Turn out on to a lightly floured board.

Knead dough, lightly pressing out into a circle about 6" (15.24cm) and place on a greased oven tray. With a sharp knife, cut two slits across the dough in the shape of a cross, about half inch (1.27cm) deep. Brush top of dough with milk and sprinkle a little flour over it.

Bake in a hot oven for 10 minutes, or until golden brown. Reduce heat to moderate and cook for a further 15 minutes.

CHOCOLATE CRUNCHIES

Warm ½oz (14.18g) margarine with 2oz (56.70g) of golden syrup and beat well. Add a pinch of salt, 1 tablespoon of cocoa or chocolate powder and beat again. Work in gradually 4oz (113.4g) rolled oats. Spread out in shallow tin and bake in a moderate oven for 20 minutes. Mark into fingers and cut when cold. Delicious!

APRICOT & NUT DIP

Ingredients:

8oz (226.80g) cream cheese, softened to room temperature

¼ cup of honey

1 cup of natural yoghurt

1 teaspoon of vanilla essence

2oz (56.70g) crushed mixed nuts

2oz (56.70g) chopped walnuts

2oz (56.70g) ground almonds

2oz (56.70g) chopped dried apricots

1 pineapple, halved, cut flesh into pieces.

Beat cream cheese until smooth. Add remaining ingredients, except pineapple, mix well. Pile into pineapple half, decorate with extra mixed nuts and dried apricots. Serve surrounded with pineapple and other fruits.

HAM TOAST

Toast rounds of bread - white or brown - to a delicate brown.

Have ready this mixture to spread on toast, heated.

1lb (0.45kg) ham finely minced, mixed with the beaten yolk of an egg, 4 tablespoons of cream and a little cayenne pepper.

Yum - Yum!!!

NUT & FRUIT CAKE

Ingredients:

8oz (226.80g) flour

6oz (170.1g) butter/margarine

6oz (170.1g) sugar

2oz (56.70g) chopped walnuts

3oz (86.05g) sultanas

3oz (85.05g) glazed cherries

1 level teaspoon of baking powder

½ teaspoon of vanilla essence

pinch of salt

Mix the flour, salt and baking powder. Chop the walnuts, cut the cherries into pieces and with the sultanas, add them all to the flour.

Cream the butter/margarine and sugar together, add the eggs, beating each one separately into the mixture.

Add the dry ingredients gradually and lastly add the vanilla essence with a little milk, if required.

Put the mixture into a paper lined tin. Bake in a moderate oven for 2 to 2½ hours. The cake should be evenly browned all over when cooked, then take out of oven and leave to cool.

SPECIAL CRISPY SALAD

Ingredients:

1 large red apple	1 large green apple
2 stalks of celery	2oz (56.70g) chopped walnuts
1 large tomato	1 small cucumber
1 lettuce	1 kiwi fruit

4 tablespoons of mayonnaise

Ingredients can be varied according to taste. Perhaps include a banana, spring or spanish onion, red beet, water melon, the choice is yours.

Wash and dice apples (do not peel). Chop the celery, slice tomato and cucumber, chop walnuts and kiwi into small pieces.

Mix all the ingredients with the mayonnaise until well coated.

Wash and drain lettuce, arrange on a plate and spoon the ingredients on top.

COCONUT BISCUITS

Ingredients:

4 tablespoons heaped with flour	1 egg beaten
2 tablespoons heaped with sugar	2oz (56.70g) margarine

1 tablespoon heaped with desiccated coconut

Mix the flour, sugar, coconut and a pinch of salt all together.

Rub in the 2oz (56.70g) of margarine and moisten with the beaten egg.

Roll out thinly and cut into shapes, your choice.

Place the shapes on a well greased and floured baking tin. Bake in a moderate oven until light brown.

FUDGE CHOCOLATE BROWNIES

Ingredients:

4oz (113.40g) plain chocolate	3oz (85.05g) margarine
5oz (141.75g) brown sugar	3oz (85.05g) plain wholemeal flour
3oz (85.05g) chopped nuts	3 eggs
1 tablespoon of essence	Icing sugar

Melt the chocolate and margarine over a very low heat in a medium sized saucepan, then remove from the heat.

Beat in the sugar, eggs and vanilla, then stir in the flour, salt and nuts.

Pour the mixture into a greased and lined 8" x 8" (20.32cm x 20.32cm) tin, and cook for 20 to 25 minutes in a pre-heated oven at 350°F, 180°C or Gas Mark 4. Do not overcook or the brownies will become hard and dry.

Allow to cool slightly, then dust with icing sugar and cut into squares.

WHO AM I? ... From Australia

I am the basis of all wealth, the heritage of the wise, the thrifty and prudent,

I am the poor man's joy and comfort, the rich man's prize, the right hand of capital, the silent partner of many thousands of successful men.

I am the solace of the widow, the comfort of old age, the corner stone of security against misfortune and want.

I am handed down to children through generations, as a thing of great worth.

I am the choicest fruit of toil. Credit respects me, yet I am humble.

I stand before every man bidding him to know me for what I am and possess me.

I grow and increase in value through countless days.

Though I seem dormant, my worth increases, never failing never ceasing.

Time is my aid and populations heap my gains.

Fire and elements I defy, for they cannot destroy me.

My possessors learn to believe in me, invariably they become envied.

While all things wither and decay, I survive.

The centuries find me younger, increasing in my strength.

I am the foundation of banks, the producer of food and the basis of all wealth throughout the world.

Yet, I am so common that thousands, unthinking and unknowing pass me by.

Anonymous Author.

No prizes - *answer at the back of the book.*

Words from Pericles' Funeral Oration over Athenians killed in war, B.C. 431. (Thucydides 111, Trans. Rex Warner)

When you realise the greatness of your city, then reflect that what made her great was men with a spirit of adventure, men who knew their duty, men who were ashamed to fall below a certain standard. If ever they failed in an enterprise, they made up their minds that at any rate the city should not find their courage lacking to her, and they gave her the best contribution they could. They gave her their lives, to her and to all of us; and for their own selves they won praises that never grow old, the most splendid of sepulchres - not the sepulchre in which their bodies are laid, but where their glory remains eternal in men's minds, always there on the right occasion to stir others to speech or to action.

For famous men have the whole earth as their memorial: it is not only the inscriptions on their graves in their own country that mark them out, no, in foreign lands also, not in any visible form but in people's hearts, their memory abides and grows. It is for you to try to be like them. Make up your minds that happiness depends on being free, and freedom depends on being courageous.

LINCOLNSHIRE AIRFIELDS
WORLD WAR II

I am indebted to Mr W.E.J. Bullock, a RAFA member at Horncastle, for helping to sort out the correct names for all the Royal Air Force operational airfields in the county during World War II. Some were known by two names and a few even had three, but we now have a complete list of 45. Unless someone knows different?

1. Bardney
2. Barkston Heath
3. Binbrook
4. Blyton
5. Caistor
6. Coleby Grange
7. Coningsby
8. Cranwell
9. Digby
10. Donna Nook
11. Dunholme Lodge
12. East Kirkby
13. Elsham Wolds
14. Foldingworth
15. Fiskerton
16. Folkingham
17. Fulbeck
18. Goxhill
19. Harloxton
20. Hemswell
21. Hibaldstow
22. Ingham
23. Kelstern
24. Kirmington
25. Kirton Lindsey
26. Ludford Magna
27. Manby
28. Metheringham
29. North Coates
30. North Killingholme
31. North Witham
32. Sandtoft
33. Scampton
34. Skellingthorpe
35. Spilsby
36. Spitalgate
37. Strubby
38. Sturgate
39. Sutton Bridge
40. Swinderby
41. Waddington
42. Waltham
43. Wellingore
44. Wickenby
45. Woodhall Spa

What is meant by some of the airfields having more than one name is illustrated by the example of Spilsby, that was also known as Firsby and Little Steeping.

The RAF had it logged as SPILSBY, because that was the nearest town. But the locals knew it as Firsby, that being the nearest Railway Station, and Little Steeping was the village close to the airfield. Perhaps the reader can now understand all the confusion caused by the airfields being called by local names by residents in the area.

Other RAF stations in Lincolnshire were used as hospitals, radio, bombing ranges and H.Q.'s including Nocton Hall, Rauceby, Theddlethorpe, Wainfleet, Holbeach, Humberston, South Elkington, Stenigot, Market Stainton, Norton Disney, Morton Hall, Skendleby, Orby, South Witham and Langtoft.

S.N.

TRUE STORY
by Ron Hawkins

"Having been in transit in the Middle East, I was posted and flew by Sunderland to Mombasa and became postman to 209 Squadron. I was the bloke who delivered the letters.

One chap was a fitter who ran the cinema once a week and brought us chunks of pineapple. The Storebasher was asleep on his bunk when he arrived one day and the fitter noticed a photograph of a girl on his locker. The fitter woke the sleeping storeman and the conversation went like this:- "Is that a photo of your girl?" "Yes" the Storeman replied. "Does her Father know you are going together?" "No, but I'll get around the old man when I get back to Blighty." "Well you'd better get around him now because that is a photo of my Daughter!"

(One never knows who one is talking to, does one? S.N.)

A SENIOR CITIZEN

A Senior Citizen is one who was here before the Pill, television, frozen food, credit cards and ball point pens. For us time-sharing meant togetherness; there were no computers - a chip meant a piece of wood or a fried potato, hardware meant durable - and software did not exist as a word. Porn meant going to uncles for a loan and teenagers never wore jeans. We were before pantyhose, drip-dry, dishwashers, tumble driers and electric blankets. We got married first, then lived together (how quaint can you be!) girls wore Peter Pan collars and thought cleavage meant something the butcher did.

We were before Batman, vitamin pills, disposable nappies, pizzas, instant coffee and Chinese take-aways. In our days cigarette smoking was fashionable, grass was for mowing and pot was a cooking utensil. A gay person was "The life and soul of the party" - nothing more, while Aids meant just a beauty treatment or help for someone in trouble.

We Senior Citizens must be a hardy bunch when you think of the ways in which the world has changed and the adjustments we have had to make to survive.

Author unknown, but given to me by a member!

I could also add that vehicles did not have automatic signals, nearside mirrors, only one rear light, no screen washers, no heaters and radios were not heard of in cars! and certainly not in lorries. However did we manage to drive from point 'A' to point 'B' and also without a mobile phone?

S.N.

MURPHY'S LAWS OF COMBAT

1. If the enemy is in range, so are you.
2. Incoming fire has the right of way.
3. Don't look conspicuous, it draws fire.
4. There is always a way.
5. The easy way is always mined.
6. Try to look unimportant, they may be low on ammo.
7. Professionals are predictable, it's the amateurs that are dangerous.
8. The enemy invariably attacks on two occasions:

    (a) When you're ready for them.

    (b) When you're not ready for them.

9. Teamwork is essential, it gives them someone else to shoot at.
10. If you can't remember, then the claymore is pointed at you.
11. The enemy diversion you have been ignoring will be the main attack.
12. A "sucking chest wound" is nature's way of telling you to slow down.
13. If your attack is going well, you have walked into an ambush.
14. Never draw fire, it irritates everyone around you.
15. Anything you do can get you shot, including nothing.
16. Make it tough enough for the enemy to get in and you won't be able to get out.
17. Never share a foxhole with anyone braver than yourself.
18. If you're short of everything but the enemy, you're in a combat zone.
19. When you have secured an area, don't forget to tell the enemy.
20. Never forget that your weapon is made by the lowest bidder.

THE GARDENER

Serene he stands amid the flowers,

And only counts life's sunny hours,

For him dull days do not exist,

Evermore the optimist.

Author unknown.

GARDENING GUIDE

1.	ALLOTMENT	Not much achieved
2.	WEED	Very easy to grow, usually the main crop.
3.	HOEING	Method of killing seedlings and flowers, whilst redistributing the stones.
4.	BROAD BEANS	Vegetables grown to feed the blackfly.
5.	PERENNIAL	Should appear each year, but doesn't.
6.	DIGGING	Wife's nagging about the garden.
7.	COMPOST	The only thing that grows.
8.	ANNUAL	An unwanted plant that persists in growing every year.
9.	ROCKERY	Heap of rubble left behind by builder.
10.	PRUNING	The finest method for killing trees.

Have a bit of fun with this diet from 'Down-Under'.

DIETING UNDER STRESS

This diet is designed to help you cope with daily pressures.

Breakfast: Half a grapefruit
1 slice wholemeal toast
300ml skimmed milk
Decaffeinated coffee

Lunch: 8oz grilled chicken breast
1 serving steamed carrots
1 cup herbal tea
1 Tim Tam *(Tim Tams are a type of biscuit. Ed)*

Afternoon Tea: Rest of Tim Tams
2 pints of ice cream
1 jar of fudge sauce
Nuts, cherries, whipped cream.

Dinner: 2 loaves garlic bread
1 large pizza supreme
6 beers
3 milky ways

Evening snack: Entire frozen cheesecake direct from the freezer while watching TV.

1. If you eat something and no-one sees you eat it, it has no calories.
2. If you drink a diet drink when eating a chocolate, the diet soft drink cancels out any calories in the chocolate.
3. When eating with someone else your calories don't count if you eat less than they do.
4. Calories in foods for medical purposes never count, e.g. hot chocolate and brandy.
5. Movie related foods do not add calories because they are part of the entire entertainment package, e.g. jaffas, buttered popcorn, minties, choc-tip ice creams, etc.
6. Biscuit pieces contain no calories because the process of breakage causes calorie leakage.
7. Things licked off knives and spoons have no calorie content if you are in the process of preparing something because calories only become part of the completed food, e.g. ice cream, icing off the knife, etc.

ENJOY YOURSELVES!

LILI MARLENE
(Pronounced "Lily Marlane")

The singer was Lale Anderson who created this great hit which became the song for both Rommel's Africa Corps, and Montgomery's Desert Rats.

The song was not a success, according to my information, until one day in 1941 a German disc jockey included the song in a programme broadcast from Budapest to Rommel's African Corps. Overnight Lale Anderson became a legend. She died in Vienna in 1972, shortly after singing the song on television that had made her so famous.

****

"Take time to work; it is the price of success.

Take time to think; it is the source of power.

Take time to play; it is the secret of perpetual youth.

Take time to read; it is the fountain of wisdom.

Take time to be friendly; it is the road to happiness.

Take time to laugh; it is the music of the soul.

Take time to love; it is the joy of life."

****

DRIVING:

    PATIENCE IS A VIRTUE.

    IMPATIENCE ON THE ROAD COSTS LIVES.

Australia

An outback Farmer waiting at the railway station, a Bible under his arm.
"Going to Sydney?" asked an old timer.
"Yairs," replied the Farmer. "Been hearing so much about them fancy Sheilas, night club shows and bikinis on the beach, I decided to go and have some fun."
"Whats the Bible for?" asked the old timer.
"Well if those Sheilas are as friendly as they say, I might stay o'er Sunday," replied the farmer.

Author unknown

Stud' Hoppers

An Australian was showing an American around his stud farm
"This is our stud ram," explained the Aussie.
"That would only be a lamb back home," observed the Yank.
"And this is our stud bull," the Aussie continued.
"Say," said the Yank, "We'd call that a calf back in the States."
The annoyed Aussie went on.
"That's our stud stallion over there," "I guess that would be a foal back home." the Yank grunted.
Embarrassed and irritated, the Australian was driving his visitor back to town when a six foot kangaroo jumped across the road.
"Hell! What's that?" exclaimed the American excitedly.
"Oh, that," replied the Aussie casually, "That's one of our grasshoppers."
Which seemed to subdue the Yank somewhat.

Author unknown.

Dave gets a "Talking To"

Dave, very dissatisfied with life on the farm, was leaving home to enlist in the permanent Army.

Mum, with thoughts of her 35 year old son exposed to the pitfalls of the big city and Army life, told Dad he'd better give the boy a "talking to".

Out behind the dairy, Dad coughed out the lecture.

"Be careful of that there liquor Dave."

"Au, I never touch it, Dad." replied Dave.

Dad proceeded with the tirade against gambling, but Dave protested he'd never wagered a penny in his life.

"Well," said Dad, "About women, now. They're a real trap for young fellas, you can land in a lot of trouble over them."

"Cripes, Dad," said Dave, "That's one thing I never do, go out with women!"

Dad went back to Mum looking rather dubious and thoughtful.

"Did you tell him?" asked Mum.

"Yairs," said Dad, "But you needn't worry, Mum, I don't think the Army will have him, the boy's a half-wit."

Author unknown

THE ROYAL BRITISH LEGION - ACT OF HOMAGE

"They shall grow not old, as we that are left grow old.
Age shall not weary them, nor the years condemn.
At the going down of the sun, and in the morning
We will remember them."

THE ROYAL AIR FORCES ASSOCIATION DEDICATION

In friendship and in service to one another, we are pledged to keep alive the memory of those of all Nations who died in the Royal Air Force and in the Air Forces of the Commonwealth. In their name we give ourselves to this noble cause. Proudly and thankfully, we will remember them.

A PRAYER

Almighty God who maketh the clouds Thy chariots, and who walketh the wings of the wind; have mercy upon all who serve in the Royal British Legion and The Royal Air Forces Association; and in their moments of need, they may have the assurance of Thy presence with them; and find Thy hand to support and strengthen them; through Jesus Christ our Lord.

Amen.

Extract from the Boston Royal British Legion 'Bulletin' May 1961

Overheard in the Club - believe it, or not!

"Not much local Branch news in the 'Bulletin' this time Fred, is there?"

"No Tom, its a thin old lot - and its a bit late out too, isn't it? You'd think they'd do a bit better with a Branch our size. I expect the Editor chap is feeling a bit tired."

"Aye, that's about it, I s'pose." said Fred. "What are you having? Its my round."

****

The pessimist sees the difficulty in every opportunity;

The optimist the opportunity in every difficulty. *L.P. Jacks*

****

Worry never robs tomorrow of its sorrows;

it only saps today of its strength. *A.J.Cronin*

****

Answers to: WHAT AM I - Land

****

In the words of Dame Vera Lynn:

"We'll Meet Again, don't know where, don't know when.

But I know we'll meet again some sunny day."

Special advertising of Museums and books by permission of the publishers

MUSEUMS

BATTLE OF BRITAIN MEMORIAL FLIGHT Dogdyke Road, RAF Coningsby, Lincolnshire, Tel: 01526 344041. Opening hours Monday to Friday 10.00am to 5.00pm. Last tour begins at 3.30pm. closed weekends, Bank Holidays and two weeks at Christmas.

On show - when not on tour - the only flying Lancaster in the U.K. Hurricane, Spitfires and a Dacota. There is a well stocked shop and refreshments are available.

THE LINCOLNSHIRE AVIATION HERITAGE CENTRE
East Kirkby, Spilsby, Lincolnshire. Tel: 01790 763207. Opening hours Monday to Saturday 10.00am. to 5.00pm. Winter closing 4.00pm. Closed Sundays.

An Aircraft Museum based on a 1940's Bomber Airfield. Displays include Avro Lancaster Bomber - none-flying but engines are operational. Original Control Tower. Wartime Blast Shelter. Air Raid Shelter. Air Craft Recovery Group exhibits, and other items on display.

Refreshments available on site, and well stocked shop.

BOOKS

AVIATION UNEARTHED.

Compiled by David Stubley, 13, Granville Avenue, Wyberton, Boston, Lincolnshire. PE21 7BY. Tel: 01205 369594.

A5 size, 80 page book with black and white photographs.

The stories behind Aircraft recoveries written by members of the British Aviation Archaeological Council.

Price £4.95 plus 50p post and packing. Make cheques payable to B.A.A.C. Post to David Stubley.

FATE HAS NO REASON.

By Chris Howard, 18, Hellesdon Close, Norwich, Norfolk, NR6 5EF.

This is an original story of a Second World War Lancaster Bomber crash that took place in the Lincolnshire Fenlands - Sibsey Northlands near Boston - where a Service is held every year on the first Sunday in October at 2.30pm.

Price £2.95 plus post and packing. Post to Chris Howard.

THE DUMMY AIRFIELD 'K' SITE HAGNABY.

By Geoff Hall and Doug Feary.

Reminiscences by the above two lads makes fascinating reading about known "DUMMY" Site that had "dummy" aircraft and clapped out vehicles in order to fool the Germans, who retaliated with wooden bombs. So much for security!

Priced at £3.00 plus 50p post and packing. Tel. 01790 753353 for further details.

50 YEARS ON - "LEST WE FORGET"

1995 Marked the 50th Anniversary of the ending of hostilities in Europe and the Pacific. In this year the Boston Ex-Services Associations commemorated and celebrated the end of the second world war in four unique events. This Video covers the highlights of two Services at the Cenotaph, a Parade and Service in the 'STUMP' and 'FORTIES NIGHT' at the Gliderdrome, in just over two hours.

Anyone can purchase the Video, of course, but it may only be of interest to people in the Boston Area.

Price £12.95 plus post and packaging £1.00 from: Harold Holdershaw, The Bungalow, Fen Road, Stickford, Boston, Lincs. PE22 8EX.

RAUCEBY REFLECTIONS

By Mrs. Gwyneth Stratten

This is the history of No 4 RAF HOSPITAL, RAUCEBY, which was operational 1940 to 1947 and had many famous names as patients including: Air Chief Marshal Sir Augustus Walker, Wing Commander Guy Gibson VC., and Flight Sergeant John Hannah, who won his VC., at the age of eighteen in 1940.

RAF Rauceby Hospital was of vital importance as it was positioned in the heart of a multitude of Lincolnshire Airfields and was therefore able to provide medical services to thousands of Service personnel.

The book is highly recommended at £2.50 plus 50p post and packing.

Post to: Rauceby Hospital, Grantham Road, South Rauceby, Sleaford, Lincolnshire NG34 8PP.